S.O.U.L.

School of Unselfish Leadership

Michael Eric Owens

S.O.U.L.: School of Unselfish Leadership

ISBN: 978-1-7332723-0-8
Copyright © 2019 by Michael Eric Owens

Published by Yes Publishing Group
A Rose Entertainment Production
29307 New Hope Rd.
Newalla, OK 74857

CONTENTS

Introduction

The *School of Unselfish Leadership* was established to develop the next generation of leaders and to improve the behavior and managerial skills of those already assuming that role. Often the myth of leadership is believed and practiced by people in charge of the livelihood of others. This myth is relied upon by those who are in fact paralyzed by their own insecurities and fragility. You will find this paralysis is very common among so many leaders today. The myth is also rooted in the idea of "position authority." The idea goes something like this: if you are in authority and have a fancy title, you are qualified to lead. This critical error is made every day in our world. I find that many company hiring practices are based solely upon qualifications and past achievements. While both of these categories should be considered, they are far from determinates of one's leadership abilities.

Furthermore, although one is an expert in a given field, it does not follow that this individual can lead. The problem with evaluating a potential candidate solely upon qualifications and achievements is the way these accomplishments make their way onto one's resume. These very flattering accolades are based upon individual attainments. Did you get that? Individual attainments… One cannot lead with the "I" complex. I am not advocating against being proud of the things we have achieved. However, leading is not an individual accomplishment. It is comprised of so many other attributes and skills, all of which are addressed in this book. Most of the time you will find that the boss is there because he or she had more experience or education, simply outlasted everyone else, or in some cases got rid of the competition... The problem lies here: Many of these individuals, who now find themselves in charge, were never mentored or trained; therefore, they tend to lead by their own selfish desires and personal agendas.

I am sure you can identify these people. You know them and more than likely at one time or another, you have worked for them or with them. Hopefully you are not one of them. But if you are, *S.O.U.L.* will deliver you. We spend most of our daily lives working and committing to a mission and a vision created by someone other than ourselves. On occasion – in a startup business, for example – we get to participate in crafting the mission and vision statements. Regardless of whether or not we played a role in codifying these, we are part of the process for achieving them. We will discuss this process in great detail.

While the missions of the companies or organizations that we work for are clear and everyone's focus should be on them, the realities are starkly different. Our focus can be skewed because workers, just like their leader, bring their backgrounds, traumas, insecurities, fragilities, and a host of other important factors to the workplace. Over time, these environments can turn toxic and become a battleground of pain and sorrow. How many tears have you shed because the boss was a narcissistic person or displayed sociopathic tendencies? I have seen many of my coworkers go to weekly therapy sessions just to have the strength to come in Monday morning. This should never be the case. When we give our all to a mission that we believe in, we should receive better in return. It is the leader's job to ensure that we are and remain in a healthy environment. An unselfish leader is a protector, a guide, a friend, and an encourager. They live to empower and rejoice in the success of those they lead. It is never about them, but about those they have stewardship over. In this book, you will learn how to be an unselfish leader and how to be successful in any situation that you find yourself in.

In my twenty-eight years of management experience, I have seen it all. Thirteen years of this experience were spent in the United States Navy. As a leader, I faced some of the most difficult challenges and managed people from all walks of life. I supervised racists, people dealing with the effects of childhood trauma, hateful and fearful individuals, and those who held extreme political views. My other fifteen years were spent in the non-profit industry where the whole goal was to serve others, yet I found that many I supervised did not really like serving others. In both of these areas, I was able to build efficient, successful, and committed teams. I was able to help them overcome their personal challenges and guide them to a more excellent way of living and appreciating those around them. I will draw on these experiences throughout this book to bring to light what it means to be an unselfish leader.

I think an unselfish leader remembers the day of his or her transformation. For me, it was aboard the Los Alamos AFDB 7 in Scotland. I had the great fortune of working for a man named Aaron Vickers. I had never met anyone like him. He was skilled, professional, and thoughtful. He was a leader who led by example. He was soft spoken, but his words spoke volumes. His team loved him and he inspired them to be more than they thought they could ever be. I was a constant observer of his leadership strategy. After a hard day's work on the Los Alamos, I would lie on my bunk at night thinking about how efficient and courteous he was. How could it be? I was so used to supervisors who were condescending; he represented the opposite. Every day I walked into a healthy environment – an environment that he created. He was a mentor, a counselor, a champion of organizational goals, and a friend.

I remember his asking me what I was doing for the weekend. I responded, "Nothing," and he invited me over for breakfast that Saturday. Little did I know he was the one making me my morning meal. For goodness sakes, my father had never made me a meal. Aaron served me as if I were an honored guest. I was further amazed by his humility. I thought for a moment – could he be human? I had never received such treatment from a manager. I felt valued and appreciated. I found him to be beyond my understanding of a leader. What was his secret? I truly wanted to know. Yet I was too afraid to ask; I was too fragile to inquire of his greatness. But I knew I wanted to be great like that. I wanted to be like him, so I watched his every move, only feeling inadequate to obtain such impeccable character.

Well, one morning, at quarters, the chief announced that Petty Officer Vickers was being promoted, and that I (Petty Officer Owens) was tasked to take over his responsibilities. Of course, no one was shocked that he'd be promoted. He was amazing. But my taking over his responsibilities was not received with enthusiasm by his team. Matter of fact, the first day I walked into the workplace as the new supervisor, it was like a funeral. People were literally crying! I thought, how can I be successful? Understand, I was new to leadership and I was in no position to be successful at such a feat. This prompted me to go to him and say, "I'm in trouble." He asked me why I was in trouble. I said, "It's a funeral in there, and I can't be you. I don't know what to do or what to say. I'm not you." He responded, "You don't have to be me. You have to be you. And I will show you everything I know."

Wow, what a powerful statement. An unselfish leader prepares and mentors other leaders for success. From that day on, he trained me, counseled me, and instructed me. This was my leadership epiphany, and I would never be the same. He was an unselfish leader, and what I have outline in this book is a guide to this platform. We can all be changed by the influence of others. I hope this is indeed your epiphany.

Let's begin…

Chapter 1
Leadership

Leadership is defined as "the ability to influence people in a positive way."[1] I want you first to notice it is called an *ability*. Now, ability is defined as "competence in an activity or occupation due to one's skill, training, or other qualification."[2] Leadership, in my opinion, is an acquired skill or training. We will come back to this in a minute. I am often asked, "Are leaders born or trained?" This is the age-old question. What do you think? I think it is easy to simply accept that either you've "got it" or you haven't. We've heard the phrase "born leader." With the very real exception of narcissists and sociopaths who have assumed leadership positions, I contend that anyone can be trained to be an unselfish leader. I think that if leadership qualities were granted simply by virtue of one's birth, and not of the ability to be developed, then we definitely would be in a famine for true leadership.

Yet I argue that certain innate qualities are essential in addition to outright training as an unselfish leader. Certainly, at the core one must possess empathy - the ability to place oneself in the position of others. You have to go beyond understanding someone to becoming someone, and the inner workings of their person must become visible to you. Let's for a moment examine invisibility. How often are you able to be yourself? You might find this to be a strange question, but it's really not. I think that through most of our lives we pretend to be what others expect us to be. An unselfish leader

[1] "4 Keys to Strengthen Your Ability to Influence Others," Center for Creative Leadership, accessed September 13, 2018, https://www.ccl.org/articles/leading-effectively-articles/4-keys-strengthen-ability-influence-others/.
[2] *Dictionary.com*, s.v., "citation," accessed September 13, 2018, https://www.dictionary.com/browse/ability?s=t.

has the ability to bring out the true you, the inner you, and the vulnerable you. The one that you are afraid to reveal because when you have in the past, you have been hurt by such exposure.

It is a fact that unless you can be open about the person that you are, you will never reach your full potential as a worker or as a person. In life, we find that there are few spaces in which we can share the true essence of who we are. Are we born with the ability to bring this out? No. We must be taught how to do this. So how does our socialization help or damage us as future leaders? Well folks, we must look back to our past and ask some tough questions: What was your childhood like? Were you fortunate to have loving and supportive parents? What were your childhood traumas? These are questions for you to answer for yourself.

In my case, I had a very harsh and demeaning father. He never had a kind word to say. He seemed to be the angriest man in the world. His father had run out on him and it damaged him. He did not have the capacity to show love or support. Yet I had a wonderful and amazing mother. She was able to compensate for his cruelty. She inherited all the qualities of an unselfish leader. She was empathic, passionate, caring, and wise. She imparted those attributes to me and taught me that life was bigger than myself. She made sure that I understood and respected the value of others and that my journey must be one of caring for and loving those placed in my life. Through the example my father offered, I learned how not to be and how not to respond to others. I had other life experiences that reinforced this notion, which I will elaborate on later.

What about you? What type of role models or mentors did you have in your formative years? We will get more into this when we discover *the power of a leader to mentor…*

So, if leadership is the ability to influence in a positive way, how do we do this? Again, I want to emphasize that it's an ability. It may be that you are reading this and saying to yourself, "I have had no positive influences in my life." Well, do not lose hope. You can still develop the ability to be an unselfish leader. I want you to be encouraged by the motto: "While I breathe, I hope."[3] You are still sitting squarely in the saddle of life and your ride is not yet finished. You can be transformed into what you have always wanted to be. The past is simply the past. It does not have to be a determinant of your future. The future is now and you are the master of your journey. So please be comforted by these words.

Unselfish leaders always look for the positive. They are corporately and individually goal oriented, meaning they have the ability to balance the expectations of the company and your future growth. They will not capitulate either for the benefit of pleasing anyone. Only by achieving success in both of these areas will they accept that their job is done. Traditional leadership is based upon results. If you hit those sales projections, if you reach so many customers, or if you have to increase your production to meet demand, then you're on the right track. Yet while results are part of the narrative, they do not write the whole story. True leadership understands that the widget is not the end-all, people are. People make the

---

[3] South Carolina's state motto

products, make the calls, interact with customers, and open and close the facilities every day, so if you invest in the people, the rest will follow.

As unselfish leaders, our personal values motivate us to invest in people. Having strong values does not alone influence people in a positive way. Those values need to take action. "An individual's values are the basic principles and tenets that guide beliefs, attitudes, and behavior."[4] When it comes to our values, we have to ask ourselves some important questions: What do I believe? How do I see the world? How do I feel about others? How do I see myself responding to others? These are just a few of the probing questions to ask. I suggest to you that we all act or behave according to the things we believe about the world and ourselves.

Furthermore, our values are seen through our social and moral lenses. The social values are freedom, equality, and world peace. The moral-based values are such things as being polite, helpful, showing affection, and having the capacity to forgive.[5] I consider the above to be core values of an unselfish leader. At times in this world, fairness can be elusive. People are truly looking for places where they can be treated fairly, where freedom and equality reside. The world is chaotic and trying to bring peace to it is a daunting task, yet we can bring peace into the lives of those we encounter daily.

---

[4] Jacqueline N. Hood, "The Relationship of Leadership Style and CEO Values to Ethical Practices in Organizations," *Journal of Business Ethics,* 43, no. 4 (April 2003): 263.
[5] Hood, 264.

In the era of diametrically opposing ideologies, religious dogma, fake news, and the death of cultural etiquette, leaders should model social- and moral-based values. What's wrong with allowing people the space to have their voices heard and validated? What's wrong with treating people equally regardless of their race, gender, socioeconomic status, or sexual orientation? What's wrong with seeking peace when conflict arises? What's wrong with being polite, helpful, understanding, and forgiving, and showing others you genuinely care about them? There is absolutely nothing wrong with operating under this value system.

When I was teaching at the Engineering School at Great Lakes Naval Base, I was called into my supervisor's office on a compliant. The complaint was that my students were laughing in my class and that they appeared to be happy. My supervisor argued, "This is the military… and sailors are meant to be hard, not soft!" Let's examine his view for a minute. He viewed human emotions being displayed by my students as being "soft." We can interpret his philosophy along these lines: a leader must rule with an iron fist to be successful. Furthermore, if your subordinates are not "serious" and not "unhappy," in his view, you are not a good leader. I'm sure you could imagine my dismay at this complaint. Let me provide a little background. These students were fresh out of boot camp. They had been in the Navy just a little over two months and were still impacted by the strict regimen of being transformed into Navy women and men. In other words, they were very fearful and timid when they arrived for their training. However, they were focused and extremely professional.

I had been in the Navy for about 10 years at this time. However, I could still empathize with these feelings and the impact it was having on the students. They were very fragile, and I saw it as my job to not only teach them, but to lead them out of this intimidating space. An unselfish leader has the ability to create an environment devoid of fear and intimidation. She can ease the anxiety of those she leads. I responded to my supervisor by stating a few facts. I pointed out that I had the highest scores of any instructor, I had more outstanding graduates at every graduation ceremony, and I had the fewest disciplinary problems throughout the entire school. His reply? "That has nothing to do with it!" Although I was sending out to the fleet the most disciplined, intelligent, and accomplished young sailors, I was a poor leader. He kicked me out of his office with these words: "Fix it."

I could not fix what was not broken. My supervisor had a different set of values than I, and many leaders you meet today fall into this category with him. Their perception of leadership is really authoritarianism. For them, there is not "we" in leadership, there is only "I." In the case of my supervisor, that leader's focus was not on the goals of the organization. Clearly, if his focus were on those goals, he would have applauded me for the success of my students and appreciated my strategy for getting them there. Rather, he saw me as weak and my leadership style as caustic to these young men and women. My supervisor lacked the capacity to see their humanity. He cared little about their well-being. In his mind was a standard definition of leadership and for him, it was the only one that counted. He was not open to thinking about leadership differently. I felt sorry for him. He had learned that authoritarian rule was the only form of legitimate leadership. During my evaluation, he gave me the lowest marks I had ever received in my military career. I was the top performing instructor with the lowest evaluation score. I took this to be a badge of honor. I knew that I was making a difference in the lives of these young people, and that was enough for me. As an unselfish leader, again, it is not about us, but about the people we help become successful.

At the end of the grading period, we always took a class photo. Upon receiving my copy, I passed it around the class and asked everyone to write something, anything they wanted - or not - about our class. Those sailors wrote the most inspirational things I have ever read. They thanked me for treating them as human. They expressed how they had come to Great Lakes broken and afraid, and that now they had hope. Many said they wished they could find someone like me out at the fleet. Some thanked me for being the father they never had… and many other kind things were written. I still pull these photos out and gain inspiration from those words today. My supervisor thought he was evaluating me. He was wrong. My students provided me all the feedback I needed to know that being an unselfish leader is worth the sacrifice. It was my goal, and it should be yours, to always influence those you lead in a positive way.

How do we influence in a positive way? Great question…

First, when we influence in a positive way, there must be a positive outcome for all involved. Second, I do not think we spend enough time contemplating how to influence those above or below us. This is an important skill to acquire. Too many times, we manage up. That is, we manage in order to please those we report *to* and neglect those who report *to us*. The saying goes, "If I keep my boss happy, then my job is secure." If this is your philosophy, then you will lose your job. No one is flawless, and to operate as a "yes" person will destroy corporate culture and result in your own destruction. In the non-profit industry, I worked for a boss that used this technique very effectively for her benefit. She was an expert at pleasing those above at the cost of those below. She had a personal agenda which was based upon her own upward mobility, and to hell with the rest of us.

I saw her methodically remove those whom she saw as a threat. If you see your employees as a threat to your success and not a contributor to it, you should not be entrusted with the livelihood of others. My coworkers walked around in fear (which, incidentally, only fed in to her narcissism). It was the only way to survive a calamitous culture. As an employee, you are powerless in a corrupt system like this. If you expressed your concern about this type of leadership, who would believe you? She had convinced everyone above her that she was an outstanding leader. Unfortunately, this is more commonly the case than not. You are seen as a tool to be used and cast aside. This is a classic example of influencing in a negative way. This so-called leader strategized to ensure a positive outcome for herself and no one else.

When we influence in a positive way, we manage down. We please those who work for us. I have to use a basketball analogy here. I'm a LeBron James fan. If I were coaching LeBron, I would ask him what he needed to win and provide that. I would ensure that he is happy with the direction of management and the team. Why? Because he is doing the work. His talent and commitment are evident. An unselfish leader recognizes the value of those doing the work. Is management doing the work? Are those above you actually doing the work? And no, I'm not advocating that you dishonor those to whom you report, but I am suggesting that you find a balance that benefits all involved. A leader understands this dilemma and responds accordingly.

Influencing in a positive way addresses the entire team. We'll examine this further when we learn how to build and maintain efficient teams, but let's entertain this notion for a moment. Unselfish leaders do not make decisions without considering the impact on the entire team. Although they know each team member intimately, they weigh each decision on its collective effect.

While I was in the Navy, I managed an engineering workspace, and at one point a man who was a racist joined our crew. He made his objection to working for a black man quite clear to his coworkers. I was immediately warned by my assistant that we were going to have problems with him. I found his predicament humorous. I was in charge and I had all the power and the support of those above me. I decided to sit down with him to understand his life's experiences. It became obvious that he'd been raised in a prejudiced environment. He was not in a personal position to receive anything that I had to offer him, so I refrained from it, simply observing him from day to day instead - a risky strategy because he could cause a lot of damage to the healthy culture I had created, yet it was worth the risk. He outwardly told me that he did not like me and did not want to work for me. I could have at any time gone to my supervisor and either punished him or removed him from my authority, but he needed me. Listen, those who are broken need empathy and not punitive action.

I recognized that his life depended upon my reaching him and helping him grow out of his restriction. I knew it was not his fault. He was only living the experience that he was given. Many years later, I would hear a conference presentation given by a professor from the University of Oklahoma. He spoke of being raised as a racist. He articulated his pain and his shame and how his adult experiences with black people had changed him. As he spoke, he began to cry, and I was so moved by his regret that I too started to cry. People have the capacity to change. We simply need to give them a chance. An unselfish leader knows this because he has been changed by his own life experiences.

For analytical purposes let's call this racists employee "Matt." Matt was nineteen years old and from a very rural community. He did not grow up alongside any minorities, and the only knowledge of them he'd obtained came from his prejudiced parents. He had created an identity of superiority over a people he had never met. The media had reinforced these skewed views through a demonization of everything black and brown. How else was Matt to feel? He had a disease and the doctor (me) was in the house. An unselfish leader does not view this as an insurmountable problem, but focuses on the great challenge to the morality of the human condition. Matt and I spent a lot of time talking and feeling each other out. Coworkers did not display the patience that I did, but that's ok. They were not in charge, I was, and it was my responsibility to reach all of them. I encouraged them to give Matt a chance and to treat him as a valuable member of the team. On occasion, it took some individual counseling with some of my team members to get them through this ordeal, but it worked. I emphasized empathy - remember this quality? I asked them to put themselves in Matt's position. I asked every one of them, "Wouldn't you want me to have patience with you?" Each one of them replied with a yes. Now they truly understood what I was trying to accomplish.

Matt gradually started to adjust to Navy life and he slowly began to change. It was not without setbacks. He went behind my back to my supervisor and complained about me, but the chief told him that he had one of the best supervisors on the ship. When the chief confronted me about it, he wanted me to reprimand Matt, but I requested he let me handle this in my way and he agreed. This is called managing down. If I were simply concerned about my career and reputation, I would have written him up, and this would have pleased my chief, but there is a more excellent way. When you manage up, you seek to please those you report to and disregard the impact your decisions have on those you lead. I sat down with Matt and talked to him about his decision to go behind my back and assured him that any complaints he had with me; we could work it out. He apologized and I felt like we had a real breakthrough.

Later, when my tenure came to an end at this command, I brought all my workers together and urged them to accept the new supervisor and press on. On my last day, Matt came to me and said, "When I met you, I didn't like you. My father was a prejudiced man and he raised me this way. After working with you for these years and the way you've treated me, there is no one on this ship I respect more than you." Matt gave me a gift that day – the gift of change. And he renewed my faith in our ability to change. I do not know what became of him, yet I believe he went on to make our world a better place. Unselfish leadership looks beyond and beneath the surface of the problem and sees possibilities. I told Matt to never blame himself for his past. I told him, "It's not your fault. You are only dealing with what was given to you." I told him I was proud of him.

I was conducting a community conversation for the Ralph Ellison Foundation, and an elderly white woman grabbed the mic and began to describe her upbringing and how she was taught to hate. She stated that each day she fights against this feeling to hate and judge. I was so inspired by her struggles and the motivation to fight and overcome. I told her, "You have said the most profound thing today. You were given something that you did not want; however, you are an overcomer, and I applaud you." We all deal with things that have been given to us without our consent. Whether or not we accept these as truth is the question. I urge you to have the courage to challenge everything you have been given. If you find it to be a worthy truth, then cling to it, but if you find it to be a lie, abandon it.

When we influence in a positive way, it is not about what we do in the moment of crisis, but how we respond. Matt became one of the most competent engineers I had and was respected by his coworkers. Remember I mentioned that influencing positively produces a situation in which everyone wins? This is not a zero-sum game. Too many leaders see it that way. Either I win or you lose. Shame on them! We can all win, if we put others before ourselves.

Who among you needs your attention and compassion?

Take a moment and list them:

_____

_____

_____

_____

Now, list the challenges and some strategies to reach them:

_____

_____

_____

_____

_____

_____

_____

_____

I personally think true leaders don't want to lead. It is a call or an elevation of one vision of humanity and their impact on the world around them. Many are called, but few are chosen. I don't believe that Dr. Martin Luther King, Jr. wanted to be the leader of the Civil Rights Movement. I think it was a call he could not refuse. I never wanted to be a leader, and certainly not to carry the burden of the livelihood of others, yet I knew it was my purpose. Jesus said, "What does it benefit a man to gain the whole world, but to lose his [S.O.U.L.]?"[6] A play with our acronym, yet applicable to our discussion. We are talking about an approach that impacts more than the individual, it borders on impacting generations. When we influence people positively, we change their lives. We help them be more than they could ever imagine.

True leadership implies that you are willing and capable of enduring staunch criticism even when it is not deserved. How many people disagreed with Dr. King? His opposition came mainly from the people of faith. He could not count on those who should have been his greatest supporters. It is the same with us. Many times, those who have hired us have no idea of what true leadership is. They have been promoted to their highest level of incompetence. So, the unselfish leader must bear the pressure of opposition. This is where integrity lives. Are you able to withstand the opposition or will you cave in? I have been under the pressure of the corporate powers and I have seen others deal with it. Again, "Many are called, but few are chosen."[7] It boils down to striking the balance. In some instances, you might lose the battle. What are you willing to lose? One must be willing to lose it all for the benefit of others. An unselfish leader will lose, yet walk away knowing that he has given it his all and done the right thing for those under

---

[6] Holy Bible: New King James Version (Chicago: Moody Press, 1985), 1552.
[7] Holy Bible: New King James Version, 1512.

him. In loss, there is great gain. You must accept and believe in this principle. If you lose, you will gain so much more for doing the right things. We carry the weight of others on our shoulders, but if you are truly an unselfish leader, you will rise again. You will rise from the ashes of depression and anxiety to a glorious dawn of a new day. You are an unselfish leader who easily pays the price to achieve greatness. Socrates said, "Be kind, for everyone you meet is fighting a hard battle." Listen, be strong and courageous and you will reach the mountain top.

"Leadership is not about a title or a designation. It's about impact, influence and inspiration. Impact involves getting results, influence is about spreading the passion you have for your work, and you have to inspire team-mates and customers." - Robin S. Sharma

the power of a leader
to mentor...

Chapter 2
Mentorship

I want to start this chapter focusing on you and end it by looking at others. Have you been mentored? One cannot be an effective mentor unless she has been mentored. You can't teach someone to play a musical instrument if you don't know how to play one. There is a great percentage of leaders today who have not had a mentor. Many simply worked their way to the top or faked their way to the top but have never truly become a student of leadership. Now, while there are many classes at universities and in the private sector on leadership, there is no substitute for practical real-life experience. In other words, you have to be a good follower before you became a leader. So many of the mistakes made by those in charge can be attributed to a lack of experience in the field of leadership. Again, your status as the most senior person, or your job title of CEO, manager, or supervisor, does not equate to being an effective leader.

In addition, just because those you supervise don't tell you that you are a poor leader, it does not mean you are a good one. They are often just too afraid to be honest with you. In many cases, people simply want to keep their jobs. I was told by the president of a company that he asked his employees to evaluate his performance, and that it turned out everyone was pleased with his leadership. The fact is, he did not see the error in his ways with such a grotesque calculation. How were they supposed to respond? Could they say, "You are doing a poor job"? "The culture here really sucks and I hate working for you"? Trust me, I knew several employees who worked there and they felt exactly that way, yet their leader was clueless of their outlook. As a leader, we must never use this strategy to gage our performance. This particular president was one of the most controlling and micromanaging leaders I have ever observed. This was a classic example of someone who had never been mentored.

It is so ironic because in the end, I got the sense that this person did not even like people. He only valued the opinion that agreed with his. This work environment was structured around his own gratification, and he bullied others into stroking his ego. The individuals who did not succumb to this brand of leadership were easily picked off and jettisoned from the workplace. I recall learning how to play basketball. I grew up in Milwaukee, Wisconsin, and the playground of choice for us was Colombia Park. It was in the hood. A very simple park with a baseball field and two basketball courts. As you entered the park through a narrow opening in the chain link fence that surrounded it, you had to walk past the dope dealers and those rolling dice for a few dollar bills. As a young child, I got used to walking past them, and they didn't seem to mind my doing so.

My friends and I would watch the older kids battle it out on the court and shoot around in between games. Most of the time, we would get their early to play before the crowd of ballers arrived. As I grew older, I found myself out there on the court taking the place of those who had moved on or found themselves housed in the criminal justice system. My point is this: I was first an observer of the sport and those things I observed; then I began to practice what I saw until I had reached a point where I could be part of a team – and even the team, of course, had a coach. It all started for me in grade school at St. Agnes. I was in the sixth grade when I tried out for the team. That year was the first time I played organized basketball. Needless to say, I was terrible, but we had one guy, Charles Berry (known around as

Chuck), who was amazing. That year he won MVP and he truly deserved it. I remember our sports banquet at the end of the season. Our coach Ben Cherry called Charles forward and presented him with the MVP award to thunderous applause from those in attendance. I was happy for him, but felt so small. At that moment I said, "That will be me next year."

I knew I had an opportunity that summer to get better, so I went to the local library and checked out a book on basketball. In this book there were illustrations on how to dibble and the proper way to shoot the ball. I knew I had to start all over, so I set up chairs in the basement of our inner-city home and dibbled around them for hours. I got to the court as early as I could and worked on my shooting form. I asked my older brother to teach me everything he knew about the game of basketball and he did. He mentored me and gave me all the knowledge he had. My brother was a gifted baseball player, but he could hold his own on the basketball court too. The following year I came back a much-improved player. In sixth grade I'd played fearfully because of my lack of skills, but in seventh grade, my confidence was evident for all to see. At that year's sports banquet, Mr. Cherry called my name and presented me with that year's MVP award.

If you want to be a good leader, you have to be a good student of leadership. You must start from the beginning. You start from a place of ignorance. That is, you accept that you lack the knowledge and skills to be effective. You're not that good! Many leaders are devoid of this level of humility. Their hubris keeps them in the space of ignorance, so they continue to go on faking it and because they are in charge, they simply give themselves the

MVP every year despite the price it is costing those around them. You must first be mentored.

To be mentored, you must first accept the reality that you do not know it all. No matter how long you have been in your line of work or the position you currently hold, you can still learn. You should possess a spirit of humility. Being humble is not a sign of weakness, but of strength. Moreover, being honest with yourself is one of the greatest qualities anyone can have. Trust me, those you lead and those around you know whether or not you are a competent leader. Secondly, you must seek out the knowledge and skills that you are lacking. Take an example from a little boy trying to get better at basketball. If you approach this with an innocence of heart, you too can become the most valuable player. Seeing Charles's success motivated me to want to be like him. His hard work caused me to work hard. I saw something in him that I wanted. The reward was just a representation of his commitment, heart, and values, which I desperately wanted.

List individuals who have presented you with great examples of hard work, commitment, humility, and values:

_____

_____

_____

_____

A mentor is a "wise and trusted counselor or teacher."[8] This is a very simple but powerful definition. It implies that one must be wise. I have found in my life that wisdom is difficult to acquire. It implies that one must learn through experiences. It is important to clarify this point. Just because you have an experience, it does not mean you have learned something from it. Some people go through life committing the same mistakes over and over again. Although they have the same experiences, they have not learned anything from them. You can go from one management position to another and continue with the same destructive practices and never change. I have just described the modus operandi of a lot of today's leaders. They don't change because they feel that they know it all. Are you a wise person? Wisdom should come with age, but it often does not. Young leaders struggle in the wisdom department. It's not necessarily a fault of theirs. They have not lived long enough to have experiences that shape their lives. Older people suffer from a lack of wisdom due to their own insensitivity to what the universe is trying to teach them.

Wisdom is defined as "having the power of discerning and judging properly as to what is true or right."[9] People often make the mistake of assuming that wisdom is acquired through the aging process. As the definition accurately points out, wisdom is a power. It is a power that accumulates greater value with each learned experience. Think of it as a bank account. Each time you

---

[8] Dictionary.com, s.v., "citation," accessed September 27, 2018, https://www.dictionary.com/browse/mentor?s=t.
[9] *Dictionary.com*, s.v., "citation," accessed September 27, 2018, https://www.dictionary.com/browse/wisdom?s=t.

go through something in life and you learn from it, you make a deposit into your wisdom account. And just as a bank account, you often have to pull from it. When you mentor someone, you are making a withdrawal from your account and transferring into theirs. It becomes problematic when the recipient (those you are mentoring) refuse to receive your funds. It can further be unsettling when wisdom is called upon, yet your account is deficient.

It is essential that you look for a mentor who has demonstrated a willingness to always do what is right and just. Your first learning is your best learning. That is, if you learn it right the first time, you won't have the struggle of breaking old habits. Few have the courage or the fortitude to relearn, and the older you get the more difficult this challenge becomes. I find myself to be among the luckiest people on the planet. I have been blessed to have had some awesome mentors. Through them I saw integrity, honesty, commitment, and fairness modeled in powerful ways. I have always prided myself on being a student of life and learning; therefore, I continue to grow as a person and a leader. I think my story is not a common one. I did not struggle with a huge ego or the notion that I knew it all. My lack of knowledge and wisdom was forever before me. My limitations spoke to me from a young age and my inability to be what I wanted to be was clear from the very start. That's why I sought out mentors to help complete me.

It is important to pause for a spell and emphasize that choosing a mentor or being a mentor is a big responsibility. You are either putting your life into someone else's hands or someone's life is placed in yours; neither position should be taken lightly. Being a mentor is not for the faint of heart. Recall it is a power, and this power must be used with caution. Too many people have been led down the wrong path by someone they looked up to. This relationship must be based on mutual trust and admiration. The teacher must teach and value the student and the student must honor and follow the teacher's instruction.

The power of discernment and judgement cannot be overlooked. How do I know what is right if I have not seen or done wrong? How can I make proper judgements if I have not made my share of mistakes? Recognizing our own fallibility is critical. It is through our own imperfections that we learn who we are and what we are – our true self. Learning how to transform our shortcomings into proper character building is key. Looking back at Matt the sailor's story, I had empathy for him because I have also been taught wrong things in my life that I took as axioms. Mentors had the patience to bring me out of my lack of understanding. Therefore, how could I not extend this understanding to him?

A main precept of unselfish leadership is understanding that you were led unselfishly too. Someone placed your needs and your success before her own. She believed in you when you doubted yourself and she demonstrated that to you. She did it because she used proper discernment and judged you positively without condemning you. She did what was right for you and did it without wanting anything in return. She did it because it was the right thing to do, and she did it unselfishly.

A mentor is not only wise, but he can be trusted. The elusive thing about trust is that from the beginning it is easily given, but once shattered, it is hard to rebuild. When that person's life is placed in your care or you freely give yourself to be mentored, trust has been established. Only a fool would get on the potter's wheel if she did trust the potter. As we mold or shape, or as we are being molded and shaped, we are vulnerable. We are open to learn or opened to be deceived, or we are open to teach or deceive. I want to be quite clear on this point: if you squander someone's trust, you will probably never get it back. Nothing in this life hurts more than being deceived or used by someone you placed your unconditional trust in. I see too many leaders fail in this area.

A leader must gain the trust of his followers. If not, you are the one deceiving yourself. You can't influence people positively without their believing in you and your values. They may work for you because they have bills, or need to put food on the table, or send a child to college, but they will eventually take their talents elsewhere.

By now I hope you have made the connection. Unselfish leaders have been properly mentored and are a mentor themselves. An unselfish leader discerns and judges and always does what is right. I found myself in a very dangerous situation in the Navy. The Engineering Chief Petty Officer demanded that I carry out an order that I knew would place him, myself, and those I managed in a life-threatening situation. When I refused to carry out the order, the room became extremely tense. He insisted that I do as he told me. I remember looking at those faces – those entrusted to me. My job was to protect them, and I knew that if I complied something bad was going to occur. Someone was wise enough to seek a second opinion on the engineering procedure, so we called the most experienced engineer on board. He arrived, assessed the situation, and said that if we do what I was told to do, we would all pay with our lives.

After this encounter was over, I was ordered to the Engineering Chief Petty Officer's office along with my boss and the expert engineer. The Chief Petty Officer was still fuming over my refusal even though I made the right decision. He said to me that I must never defy him, especially in front of subordinates. I apologized to him for the way it made him look, but I refused to apologize for making the correct decision. At this, he started yelling at me and told me, "You never let those junior to you know you don't know something." I guess he would rather die than be wrong. Well, I was not willing to embrace such a fate. Do you think I trusted him after that incident? Do you think my workers trusted me after this? At that moment, I was not concerned about my career. I was only concerned about my crew and the lives under my charge. Of course, my life was important, but not my career. Now, you might think my decision was a career-ending one. Well, it wasn't. The Engineering Chief Petty Officer was eventually replaced, and I would go on to receive the Sailor of the Year award from that command. My workers celebrated with me. It was our award, and one of the greatest honors of my life.

Hopefully you are never called to make a decision of that magnitude and with those consequences, but you will be called to stand in difficult situations on behalf of those you supervise. This story had a silver lining; however, I have had my share of negative outcomes simply for doing the right thing. Discouraging as this may sound, receiving a positive outcome should never be a condition for choosing to do the right thing. You do it because it is right. If we canvass history, we will find that a lot of great leaders stood alone, paid a price, were demonized, ostracized, and abandoned; and yet the world is a better place because of their sacrifices. They were unselfish in their stand for truth and justice. Take great comfort in knowing that there have always been and continue to be those among us who lead on principle, unwavering and faithful to their mission. What are you willing to lose for the sake of others? You cannot be an unselfish leader if you are not willing to lose for the empowerment and success of others. This is a hard saying, I know, but a truthful one. If you are given the leadership charge, you are responsible for the lives of others. You are entrusted with their futures, dreams, and aspirations. You are the potter and they are your clay. You are required to mold them in a positive way. They are looking to you for guidance and direction, and you must never let them down. And if you do, you work to rebuild and regain their trust…

An unselfish leader is a wise and trusted counselor. In other words, you are a great listener. This is a lost art in our society. In the information age, our attention span continues to decrease. With the rise of social media, we have less face-to-face interaction. The days of long, in-depth conversations are gone. We simply want people to get to the point and move on to the next task. The idea of engaging in meaningful dialog is archaic to some. Yet, as an unselfish leader, your time belongs to those you lead. Listening is a key ingredient in a mentor's recipe book. My mother was a great cook and she loved baking. We were seldom without something sweet in the house. She took great pride in providing these treats for her family. One day I was assisting her in the kitchen to make a cake. I noticed that she measured nothing. She asked me to add some baking power to the bowl and I asked her where the measuring spoons were. She began to laugh and said, "You have a lot to learn! Boy, give me that baking powder." She knew exactly what was needed and how much. Why? She had baked this cake many times before. She was an expert.

As a mentor, we should know how much dialog is needed and how much is required for those we direct. Like my mother, our experiences will prepare us for the next one and then the one after that. This is why being mentored is so important. Once the student becomes the teacher, he simply teaches. Once we have been reached or apprehended ourselves, we know how to reach others. Our keen insight will guide them out of all the challenges they face. Unlike a cookbook recipe, life does not have step-by-step directions. Our past experiences and the things we have learned from them are our blueprints. Are you confident in the things you have learned, and if so, can you use those things to mentor others? If not, the school of life is still accepting applications, and it has no age restrictions.

List things you have learned that will help you mentor others:

_____

_____

_____

_____

_____

_____

_____

I want to turn your attention back to listening. My mother was my first and most powerful mentor. She was a dynamic leader. She lived an unselfish life and taught others through her words and example how to achieve such a fulfilled life. I recall one time when my mother was having a difficult time with her boss at her job. She was sharing some of this with me when I asked her what she was going to do about it. She said, "Well, he's a big cigar, but I can smoke him." We both laughed, but it reminds me of how she viewed challenges. She believed that she would overcome and not be overcome. How much do you remember from those who have mentored you? Were you listening? In a mentor relationship, listening requires that we hear, interpret, and apply. We must never forget what has been passed on to us. Although her boss was in control, she was in control of her response and most importantly, she controlled the burn. Lastly, a cigar does not burn forever – so remember, challenges will eventually come to an end too.

A counselor also knows when and when not to offer advice. If you have ever been in counseling or assumed the role as counselor, you know that listening is your greatest offering. You are leading people who want to do their best. Many times, these individuals are looking for direction and they have a burning desire to please you. You are a role model and you exemplify success for them. Often, they are hoping to be in your position one day. The experiences you have had and the things you have had to overcome still lay ahead of them. A counselor draws upon these experiences and slowly guides his subject through these mazes. If you do not listen or if you are pressed for time because you simply want them to get back to work, you are losing out on a life-changing episode for them.

I once managed an operation in which two key people despised each other. They shared job responsibilities and were both extremely passive aggressive. After being in charge for a short time, it quickly became clear that they had been operating like this for years. Both were unhappy and faced each workday with gloom. There was no trust between the two and they were there simply because they needed jobs. I believe deep down inside they were hoping to outlast the other person. I brought them in one at a time and tried to understand their history together, and it didn't take long before I discovered that this rivalry had taken on a life of its own. Each felt that she had been wronged by the other and neither one wanted to work together. Their relationship was comprised of years of hurt feelings, rumors, mistrust, and deception. While I recognized that the current problem existed between them, each of their personal lives played a part in it.

For starters, there were cultural and racial differences that had never been appreciated. Both had been hurt in the past by coworkers, and they entered the work relationship with mistrust and skepticism about the other person's motives. I brought them in my office and shared many of my observations. I expressed how I wanted them to be successful and how valued they were to the organization and personally to me. I told them it took years for them to get to this point; therefore, it will take some time to develop a healthy work relationship. I asked them if they were willing to work with me on improving this situation. I assured them that I had both of their interest at heart, and I guaranteed them we will be victorious together. Without enthusiasm, they agreed to give it a shot.

I started off by giving them some information on conflict resolution. I assigned specific readings for them, and we met individually and then collectively, weekly. I became their counselor, and I was honored to take on this role. We stayed on conflict resolution for the first month and together we came up with strategies to deal with rising problems. The first month was really intense and several tears were shed. They got to the point where they felt comfortable openly talking about the ways they felt hurt by each other. These were powerful moments in their process towards healing. Everyone enters counseling because something is broken. How to fix what is broken is the central question.

From there we went on to spend an entire month on communication and proper listening skills. One would think that listening is not a skill. We have two ears and thus we are biologically equipped to receive information; however, listening is a process. It involves the mind, heart, and patience. In other words, I have to process and internalize it, and ultimately wait long enough for this to happen to respond intelligently. Oftentimes we are thinking about what we are going to say next and we are interpreting the information with our own biases. Listening with empathy is the key. When we listen with empathy, we value the feelings of others. Although we might not agree with their perspective, it is truly their perspective and it's worthy of our contemplation. It's important to know that cultural differences play a major role in how we communicate and interpret the things spoken to us. I will admit that cultural competency training is beyond the scope of this narrative, so I encourage you to research this growing literature.

In all, we spent six months in counseling. The majority of our conversations did not include any workplace tasks. They were mainly focused on the baggage they brought to work and their interpersonal reactions to each other. In the end, trust was not completely there, but they were standing on a foundation that could eventually build trust. In the coming years, I saw them thrive in their jobs and together they exhibited respect for the other. When I moved on from that position, they expressed deep appreciation for my efforts and belief in them. As an unselfish leader, I recognized that not all of my employees needed this type of attention or intervention, yet when you are committed to the culture you are trying to create, you will do what is necessary not to leave anyone hurting on the periphery.

A mentor is also a teacher. Yet this gets us back to our original idea of the mentee. A teacher should have been taught. One of the greatest qualities of life is remaining teachable. A wise person knows when he is the teacher and when he is the student. As a mentor, you are the instructor of someone's life. A teacher knows that the "... wisdom I've collected over the years is not my personal property."[10] This is a very important principle. We are not the originator of knowledge; we are the carrier of knowledge. Too many leaders are afraid to share what was given to them out of fear of being overshadowed. A teacher must never be timid or fearful. These are selfish and weak qualities. Remember, we are talking about an unselfish leader. Sharing one's knowledge shows humility and a desire to elevate those following you.

The apostle Paul stated, "For I delivered unto you first of all that which I also received, how that Christ died for our sins according to the scriptures."[11] Paul as a leader shared the knowledge he received. A great teacher is first and foremost a learner. We absorb as much information as we can and then we become a conduit to our students. When I taught at the university, it was my job to educate and equip a new generation of learners. Why would I withhold the things I have been taught? One of the main reasons we learn is to pass it on to others. A mentor is a wise teacher. She recognizes that every encounter with a mentee is an opportunity to impart valuable information. It's quite arrogant to treat knowledge as a personal possession. The world is filled with information and the only reason to acquire it is to apply and distribute it.

---

[10] Richard F. Collins. "Mentorship as a Responsibility: Two Thirties for One Fifty," Journal of Environmental Health 69, no. 2 (September 2006): 4.

[11] Holy Bible: King James Version, 1779.

However, you can never be an effective mentor without building an unconditional relationship with those over whom you have stewardship. It is only through a trusting relationship that we find the opportunity to build people up, but the opposite can be true. If we are crafty and seek our own agenda, we can destroy people. An unselfish leader is in the business of building people up, developing new leaders, and finding satisfaction in the success of others. When a group of senior leaders was asked the reasons for their greatest success, they responded by saying it was solid relationships that caused their career ascensions.[12] Being able to view one's success as being built on the advice and direction given by others is another principle to learn. No one is an island unto himself. We require the most delicate care and guidance. If I trust you, I will follow you. If I do not, I will run from you. Sharing our knowledge makes us an intellectual magnet attracting those thirsting for it. At one time, you were looking for that teacher, that mentor, and that leader to deposit what was lacking in your life, and you can be that for someone else.

Scenario: *Mentorship*

You recently accepted a new position in which you supervise two managers. One manager is humble and is looking forward to your leadership. The other manager was a candidate for the position you filled (of course, you found this out after you accepted the job). Let's call this second manager Phyllis. Phyllis has been with the company for 15 years, and she believes she should

---

[12] Ted Mitchell and Michael Rao. "Mentoring and Peer Relationships: Two Young Leaders' Perspectives," Change 30, no. 2 (January – February 1998): 46.

have been offered the job. She is also convinced that she knows more about the job and company than you, and that she knows best how to run the departments. Yet people in these departments, and the other manager, do not view Phyllis this way. They think she is arrogant, harsh, and a know-it-all. You have overheard Phyllis making such accusations to other employees regarding you.

It is apparent that Phyllis is not interested in having a mentor, but your other manager is. How do you begin a mentoring relationship with your willing manager when Phyllis is creating a toxic environment? Do you address this issue of Phyllis being passed over for the job with her before you invest in your other manager? Is mentoring out of the question until you have created a positive work environment?

What would you do?

_____

_____

_____

_____

_____

_____

_____

_____

_____

"You can build a much more wonderful company on love than you can on fear." - Kip Tindell, Former CEO, The Container Store

Chapter 3
Diversity

There has been a lot of talk about creating diversity in leadership over the past twenty years. Diversity has become a buzz word with multiple meanings. There are countless diversity programs out there, yet I'm convinced that many people have no idea what true diversity is. At its basic level, many perceive diversity as blending together people of different races. Oftentimes it is not a true mix. You frequently find the majority of the staff are white with perhaps one of the following: a Black, Asian, or Hispanic person. After achieving this amalgamation, the organization or company calls it a day and that diversity policy gathers dust in the ole employee handbook. Diversity is much more complicated than that.

Diversity is defined as "the inclusion of individuals representing more than one national origin, color, religion, socioeconomic stratum, [and] sexual orientation."[13] An unselfish leader is aware of these complexities and happily takes on the challenge of creating a diverse team. I find that most leaders have a problem understanding the meaning of "inclusion". We live in a society that is dominated by one racial group. It would not be as problematic if this group did not maintain the levers of power in our country, but they do. Look at any corporate board room and you will notice that most leadership teams are comprised of white males. From the origin of this country, this has and continues to be a fact. Sprinkled among them might be a minority person, but most would view this leadership as normal. Why do you think this is accepted as being normal?

---

[13] Dictionary.com, s.v., "citation," accessed November 12, 2018, https://www.dictionary.com/browse/diversity?s=t.

I assert that this is the old normal. The demographics of our country are rapidly changing and our leadership should reflect this change. In the 1980s, the phrase was "We need to learn to tolerate each other." Toleration is not inclusion. I have come to despise that word. The idea that you need to tolerate someone who is different from you is insulting. The definition of tolerate is "to allow the existence, presence, practice, or act of without prohibition or hindrance; permit."[14] Who has the control here? Who decides to allow you to exist, practice or act? You are here only because I have allowed you to be. You can speak only because I have allowed it. Yes, you can do that only because I have granted you permission. It sounds very paternalistic. The idea of toleration keeps those deemed "outsiders" in a perpetual childlike state – seeking the approval of others to be who and what they are.

Now, let me introduce the concept of coexisting. To coexist means "to exist together at the same time or in the same place."[15] This asserts that I belong here just as you do. It's not your place. It is our place. How can we have a healthy relationship if you tolerate me in your space? We can't... A relationship based on tolerance involves power dynamics. It implies a hierarchy. We can look at power dynamics this way: different people or different groups of people interact with each other, but one of these sides is more powerful than the other. Throughout American history, those most powerful and those with access to resources have advocated a society based

---

[14] Dictionary.com, s.v., "citation," accessed January 5, 2019, https://www.dictionary.com/browse/tolerate?s=t.
[15] Dictionary.com, s.v., "citation," accessed January 5, 2019, https://www.dictionary.com/browse/coexist?s=t.

on tolerance. Oftentimes they unwittingly espouse this philosophy not understanding the structures at play. If a leader creates an environment or culture in which tolerance is key, he has established a ruling class and a subjugated class in the workplace. This is an unharmonious relationship and soon chaos, mistrust, and ostracism reign.

Coexisting speaks of us being synced together in harmony. Think about the last time you heard a fine *a cappella* choir performance. Not one voice stood out above the others. It was the perfect display of synchronization. So must be a diverse and coexisting environment. Imagine the attitude of a band that simply tolerates one of its members' existing or adding her part to it. This sounds kind of ridiculous. This is because they in fact depend on each other to perform well. I think you can understand where I am going here. As a leader who is focused on building a diverse team, you must always place the highest priority on ensuring that everyone understands and buys into a coexisting philosophy. Many times, in work teams, people do not even feel that they are being tolerated, much less that they are in coexistence with others. So, the next time someone mentions to you that we should tolerate each other, I hope you take that as a cue to create a teachable moment.

As an unselfish leader who builds diverse teams that coexist, you will find that at the core of this endeavor lies the ability to include a diversity of informed opinions. I want to emphasize "informed" opinions. An opinion is only of value when it is steeped in an understanding of the topic. Listen, I am not a cardiologist, so please do not ask my opinions as they relate to the human heart. As a side note, always be informed before offering an opinion. Opinions are shaped by so many factors such as our parents and upbringing, where we grew up, other experiences and things we have been exposed to, just to name a few. And because of these factors, not everyone will share the same opinions. Learning to solicit, include, and rely upon ideas and input requires an interest in others, and often patience.

If you do not find people interesting and you are short in the area of patience, you will not be successful at including a diversity of opinions. Plus, diversity of opinions is the opposite of group think. The majority of my professional life has been spent in groups that simply want you to think and act alike. A leader that has created a homogeneous group will despise anyone that deviates from the shared opinion of the group. It is important that you recognize quickly the group you are involved in. You will find that it is more important what a leader does than what she says. The principles we are talking about in this chapter can be found in every strategic planning document out there; however, most of them are merely words on a page lacking completely in application.

If I have a different opinion about an issue that we are debating, does that make me your adversary? Strange question? I think not… Oftentimes, those who share a different viewpoint are seen as an adversary. More than likely you are viewed as an enemy of the group. You will encounter such complaints as "He always disagrees," or "She thinks she knows it all." In addition, many fragile leaders are threatened by individuals who are confidant in their opinions. That time I shared my opinion in the Navy, I was told, "Just do as I told you to do." In the end, the opinion I had saved the Navy over a million dollars, yet my superior was too proud to admit his mistake.

As an unselfish leader, you invite diverse opinions. You not only welcome them, but you require them. Having a different viewpoint is celebrated not just from the leader, but within the team. How about saying something like this: "I never thought about it that way," or "That's a great way of looking at it," or "I will definitely consider that." People feel valued when they feel accepted. You are the leader and your staff are looking up to you. They look up to you for guidance and for validation.

I want you to embrace the concept that even before people offer their opinion, individual diversity of thought must be appreciated by you. Our thought process is complicated and sometimes certain people have difficulty articulating their thoughts. In some cases, the words may not come out right. Have you heard someone say, "I just don't like the way he said that?" There is a deep problem in that statement and we will examine it when we look at dealing with conflict later in the book. However, a leader must start with the premise that everyone wants to add value to the conversation. This premise is based upon the assumption that most people have good intentions and that we all make mistakes from time to time. Keep in mind, some conversations can trigger a bad experience or a childhood trauma, so being patient in these situations is mandatory. With those who are quick witted, praise them, and for those who struggle with the right words or approach, coach them and still praise them.

Diversity can be observed in many different ways. Even when you have a diverse team along racial, ethnic, and gender lines, there are other depths of diversity such as diversity of gestures, for example. On the surface, this may seem quite silly, yet non-verbal communication is more powerful than the words we speak. For instance, there was a time in my career in which my passion was interpreted as being aggressive. I can be somewhat expressive with my hands, and someone not used to this type of communication style saw it as intimidating. Of course, I was criticized for my hand motions instead of our supervisor helping the offended person understand that not everyone is a laid-back communicator. When tension like this arises, a good leader sees this as a teachable moment. Unfortunately, I had to capitulate this aspect of my personality to appease this one individual. The supervisor and this team member dictated my communication style moving forward. I was allowed to participate according to their rules. Therefore, I was being tolerated.

This leader should have asked questions like, "What about his communication intimidates you?" Or, "How does his communication style make you feel?" Furthermore, this leader should have brought us together and begun a dialog between us concerning his issue with me. When you coexist, it means that my communication style has every right to be an equal component of the conversation. Now, let's be clear: I'm not talking about abusive language, yelling, verbal intimidation or the like. I'm simply talking about different communication styles. We need to understand that our body language and mannerisms can be different depending on our upbringing, cultures, country of origin, and a host of other factors. There is not a one-size-fits-all box that we check when we coexist.

When it comes to creating an atmosphere where diversity can flourish and people can coexist, creating a healthy workplace culture is essential. This is without a doubt the most important step towards building efficient and diverse teams. Culture is defined as "the behaviors and beliefs characteristic of a particular social, ethnic, or age group."[16] Notice the definition states that culture relates to a specific group. No two organizations' cultures are the same. You might discover similar characteristics, but they will not be identical. That is, each of us play a part in creating and maintaining a specific culture. Such things as trust, acceptance, how we deal with conflict, and defining roles and responsibilities are a few of the characteristics of a workplace culture. We will deal specifically with this in the culture chapter. Keep in mind that several members of an organization might be coming from very different communities or work cultures, yet we must find a way to blend into one distinct work culture. Without creating a healthy work culture, true diversity will never be achieved.

Achieving diversity must be a priority in an organization. The steps taken to create such a place should go beyond the micro organizational level. The top leaders must embrace this effort and ensure that everyone buys in.

> The successful development of a diversity-sensitive organization is significantly different from increasing the percentage of minority representation. It requires senior leadership— starting with the CEO—to openly commit to the recruitment, retention, development, and support of candidates previously underrepresented. The leadership must educate and convince others that this is of strategic value and is the long-term direction of the organization. The CEO should recognize that those resisting this process will wait for a decrease in attention and prioritization on this effort and hope to see it die a natural death. It is his or her responsibility

---

[16] Dictionary.com, s.v., "citation," accessed February 12, 2019, https://www.dictionary.com/browse/culture?s=t.

to maintain the focus and make it easier to comply and participate than resist.[17]

As an unselfish leader you must articulate the advantages of inclusion. You set the tone in your organization and you are the creator of culture. Diversity is truly a commitment to people, equality, equal opportunity, and social justice. It takes a special leader to understand the impact that diversity has on an organization. A leader who comprehends the past, the ills of society, and the measures needed to create a more equitable world, knows the importance of diversity. Knowing that everyone deserves a seat at the table should be a motivating factor for today's leaders. Creating a diverse company requires constant attention to ensure its success.

Establishing fair hiring practices, promoting equitable participation in the day to day operations, and ensuring opportunities for promotion all require a hands-on approach. Holding your Human Resource Department, directors, managers, and supervisors accountable is only the beginning of compliance. It is much easier, though less productive, to create homogeneous teams than diverse ones. A researcher's findings indicated that leaders of homogeneous teams ranked themselves higher than leaders of diverse teams. The diverse group leaders rated themselves lower because they encountered socioemotional conflict "because of style differences and perceptions of interpersonal biases. These leaders find themselves having

---

[17] Janice L. Dreachslin, "The Role of Leadership in Creating a Diversity-Sensitive Organization," Journal of Healthcare Management 52, no. 3 (May/June 2007): 151.

to deal with these conflicts to ensure a well-functioning team."[18] In homogeneous groups, leaders received feedback that mainly supported their ideas, perceptions, and worldview. In other words, they created an environment in which everyone agreed with them, often referred to as a "yes environment."

Fragile leaders have a difficult time handling disagreements or dissent. They surround themselves with "yes" people to stroke their egos. Often in situations like this, there is little to no accountability for this type of leader. They simply "manage up." They please their supervisor or their board of directors and intimidate those who work under them. Since those above them are satisfied and disconnected from the day-to-day operations, workers feel powerless to speak up because of retaliation from the boss. I have found that leaders who are sociopathic or narcissistic conduct business in this way. As a side note, I suggest you do some research on sociopathic and narcissistic behaviors. In life, you will meet people like this from time to time. You might unwisely marry one. However, I contend that most of us will eventually work for one, so knowing what you are dealing with is key to your survival. These are two dangerous qualities found in too many leaders today. I hope that you are not one of these types, because this speaks to a much deeper problem than this narrative could ever solve.

Leading diverse groups is challenging work. This is why so few exist throughout the workforce. However, unselfish leaders are trained for this

---

[18] Janice L. Dreachslin, "The Role of Leadership in Creating a Diversity-Sensitive Organization." 152.

task and they welcome the job of building diverse teams without hesitation. Although you may work in the Tech industry, or Education, or Law Enforcement, you are in the people business. Individuals make up the workforce. Therefore, where we lead them, they will follow.

Here are three ways you can begin to become a Diversity Leader:

1. Friends: Expand your inner circle beyond your own demographic and observe what you think, what you feel, and how you respond as you invite diverse individuals in. Research supports the contention that leaders who experience diversity in their personal lives are more diversity sensitive than those who do not.
2. Experiences: Put yourself in the minority – and not the power – position and watch your own reactions. A proven exercise in empathy, personal experience with minority status is also associated with Diversity Sensitive Organization (DSO).
3. Executive coaching: Consider developing a confidential relationship with a professional who allows you to safely disclose and explore areas for improvement in your DSO that might feel too risky to discuss in a public forum such as a diversity training.[19]

---

[19] Janice L. Dreachslin, "The Role of Leadership in Creating a Diversity-Sensitive Organization." 153.

Who's in your inner circle? Are there people of color? Women? Name a few:

_____   _____

_____   _____

_____   _____

_____   _____

What's your definition of empathy?

_____

_____

_____

_____

_____

I urge you to establish a relationship with an executive coach. The investment is minor, but the reward is great. I advise many leaders today, and it has always been a rewarding experience. If you are looking for an executive coach, contact me and I will get you on the right track.

If you don't step outside of your comfort zone, you will never understand the experiences of others. Too many people in the workplace feel ostracized and isolated. They are there simply because they have to pay the bills. It's not about production or performance. It's about survival. How can we strive if we are always only trying to survive? Think about that new hire and the enthusiasm that person displays arriving for the first day of work. They have expectations, dreams, goals, and aspirations. They are looking to you to support and guide them as they carry out the work you have tasked them to do. But how quickly all of these positive impulses can be shattered.

You hired a whole worker and now he is broken because of a dysfunctional culture. I think we often forget that the worker's contract is twofold. The leader and the worker both have an obligation to fulfill their respective parts of the contract, but I seldom find this to be the outcome. The leader fails and expects the worker to be content with her failure. Too many in this field are eager to push the team member out and start over again with their next victim.

Any discussion about diversity would be incomplete without addressing *White Privilege*. There is a reason that diversity is a lofty goal in our society. It is because of a history of exclusion among the races. From the origins of the United States, there has been a need to place value upon one's race or, should I say, skin color. Slavery, Native American removal, Jim Crow and the like were only achievable by devaluing the lives of non-Europeans. For a long time in America, white people dominated its landscape. A system of racism was created and, some would argue, maintained by those in power to this day. When you canvass early American leaders, minorities and Native Americans are not included among them. For most of its history, the United States also excluded women from leadership roles.

All but one of the American presidents has been white, and congresspeople, judges, CEOs, and leaders in local and state governments on down to blue collar managers have been white males. In other words, these individuals have been in charge and the concept of diversity of leadership implies that now they have to share power, and, in some cases, relinquish areas of power to people who were never intended to lead in American society. There is still a segment of this society that refuses to embrace diversity and instead views it as an assault on their standing in this country. Some view diversity as reverse racism, and others have gone as far as to call it un-American.

Seth Grossman, a GOP candidate in New Jersey's 2nd Congressional District said, "The whole idea of diversity is a bunch of crap and un-American."[20] This congressional candidate clearly does not understand the definition of diversity; however, he is right on one account. American systems were created to benefit one group over the other. The constitution was written with high ideals, but in its application, it gave advantages to whites over all other groups. Ironically, here is a man that is running for a leadership position in our government. How many feel the way he does, but are simply too afraid to say it? He cannot be the only one espousing these ideas. How would you like to be a minority person among his staff? Do you think you would feel included and valued as a team member?

---

[20] Lydia O'Connor, "Diversity is A Bunch Of Crap And Un-American,' Says GOP Congressional Candidate," Huffington Post, June 11, 2018. https://www.huffpost.com/entry/seth-grossman-diversity-unamerican_n_5b1eaab9e4b09d7a3d7596f9.

It is important to acknowledge that the United States never got the equality education it so desperately needs. Racial differences are social constructs are used to elevate one group of people over all others. It's a big lie on which so many have based their identity. Even those in the underclass have bought into this false reality. How else can a minority person be highly educated, wealthy, live in an affluent neighborhood, and hold an esteemed job and still be viewed as inferior to a white person who is poor and uneducated? It's called white privilege. This single idea that my skin has less pigment than yours implies that I am superior. It's a funny concept when you view it through the scenario I just mentioned. These grotesque misconceptions play out every day in America, and especially inside your work group.

These differences are taught daily. They are overt in news media, film, and across socio-media platforms. One example is that most heroes in movies are white males. Even in the movie *The Last Samurai*, the hero is white. It is based on a true story; however, the role of Tom Cruise is greatly embellished. The bottom line is that white privilege is prevalent in the workplace. One must first acknowledge that it does exist, and then educate staff when conflicts arise about white privilege. Inherent in white privilege is an unconscious sense of an entitlement. You should assume that minorities are aware of white privilege, but not necessarily your white staff. White privilege can be defeated in the work environment by including everyone, giving equal weight to ideas and interests, and applying workplace rewards and justice fairly.

Lastly, the benefits of workplace diversity are proficiency, maximum creativity, minimum employee turnover, and a healthy work culture.

Everyone wants to do a good job and be appreciated for it. Diverse group complement each other. The blending of apparent differences should be seen as a strength, and this will build stronger teams. Further, becoming proficient at one's job requires learning, and the best learning is achieved from learning from one another. Beyond being excluded, people leave a job because they feel stagnant. The creative juices have ceased to flow. When everyone feels part of a mission and knows her role, she has the room to be creative. When his ideas are accepted and implemented, it produces more creative responses. People simply don't want to leave a job they are happy in. Work is fun and purposeful for them. It becomes part of their contribution to society. A happy and content worker will follow wherever you lead. Remember, culture is key. We will get into the dynamics of a healthy culture in a later chapter, but for now, you need to know that culture is shared and maintain by all involved.

How can you create diversity as a leader?

_____

_____

_____

_____

_____

_____

_____

_____

_____

_____

_____

When have you seen diversity work and how?

_____

_____

_____

_____

_____

_____

Scenario: *Diversity*

One morning as you enter the office, you see Jessica walking in and you say, "Good morning Jessica, how are you?" "I'm not doing so well," she replies. You ask her to step into your office and take a seat. "What seems to be the problem?" "I don't feel like I'm being treated fairly by others in the office. I don't know if it's because I'm a female or a Latina, but I'm treated differently." Jessica goes on to provide some evidence to you involving, for example, emails and conversations; and she identifies those individuals causing her to feel this way.

What do you say and what suggestions to you give moving forward?

_____

_____

_____

_____

_____

_____

_____

_____

_____

_____

_____

_____

_____

_____

_____

_____

_____

In Auguste Renoir's classic painting *Woman with a Parrot*, we see a young woman gazing downwardly at her bird whose feathers of black, white, brown, green, red, and soft shades are blended into utter unison. To remove a tone would render Renoir's piece imbalanced and unsynchronized. Life is truly art. Creation generously reveals its own magnificence. The palette of the changing seasons, the rhythm of the forest wind, the stillness of the river valleys, and the appearance of the rainbow after the storm all show us that God Himself prefers variety to create beauty. Life is truly art, and to suggest that diversity is un-American continues to this day to render America imbalanced.

Chapter 4
Conflict

At one point or another, we will experience conflict in our lives. Whether it's in our personal or professional lives, we will find ourselves at odds with others. So, it's not a question of whether it will happen, but when will it happen. I am sure you have heard that not all conflict has to have negative outcomes. The impact of these episodes of conflict depends on the actors involved and our responses to it. Most people have difficulties addressing and responding to conflict. I think we are biologically engineered to run from disagreements and retrieve to our safe places; however, there is no growth in this practice.

Conflict is described as to come "into collision or disagreement; be contradictory, at variance, or in opposition; [to] clash."[21] Conflict and collision are a powerful linguistic pairing, and for some, conflict can prove fatal. It is important to distinguish between intrapersonal conflict and interpersonal conflict (in which physical harm is caused by another). These types of episodes are unhealthy and must be avoided at all cost. So, I am not insinuating that these conflicts should be dealt with in the same way workplace conflicts should. Interpersonal conflict can have deadly outcomes, and hopefully no conflict in the workplace will reach this level. Because of true diversity, differences of opinion will arise from time to time. We must not avoid them or treat them as fatalities.

Besides, who would want to coexist will people who think alike, believe alike, and always share the same opinions? Think of a world in which

---

[21] Dictionary.com, s.v., "citation," accessed March 16, 2019, https://www.dictionary.com/browse/conflict?s=t.

everyone acted the same, talked the same, and reasoned the same. I think this would be a boring world. Where would our inspiration come from? Where would innovation and creativity start and end? We truly need different worldviews to keep our world turning and progress blooming. Let these be some of your thoughts the next time you face conflict.

Is it possible to view conflict in a positive way? As much as these situations can cause discomfort and level a blow to the human heart, the other side of conflict can be greater creativity, production, and innovation. Research had uncovered that "conflict has been linked to learning, to higher levels of creativity and innovation, to improved quality of group decision-making, and to increase overall team effectiveness."[22] So for starters, not all conflict is destructive. Some scholars believe that conflict is quite desirable, should be welcomed and, where possible, stimulated.[23] Although this can be easier said than experienced, allow me make my point.

While there are many reasons that conflict arises in an organization, I want to concentrate on the most obvious ones: *task-related conflict* (TRC) and *relationship conflict* (RC). In my personal experiences, RCs have occurred more often than TRCs. When we talk about RCs, one must factor in the ego, power dynamics, and the pure need to excel above others, while discounting the value of other team members. TRCs are conflicts about the way people are doing their jobs. RCs are conflicts related to people, their values, their

---

[22] Crasten K.W De Dreu, "The Virtue and Vice of Workplace Conflict: Food for (Pessimistic) Thought," *Journal of Organizational Behavior* 29, no. 1.(2008): 5.
[23] Ibid.

humor, etc.[24] Now that you know the difference between the two, which one, in your opinion, occurs most often? Relationship conflicts are truly hard to understand and address.

Looking back on our diversity chapter, I hope you can imagine that the gathering of a diverse team would lead to some measure of RC. As a matter of fact, it should be expected. You are blending people of different backgrounds, experiences, cultures, and ethnicities, so there will be episodes of disagreement and tension. An unselfish leader uses these instances as teachable moments. He looks upon this as an opportunity to educate, not alienate. Let's use a silly analogy... Have you ever made smoothies? You can start by placing different types of fruit into the blender, and then add milk, flax seed, and possibly greens. You push the power button and all the separate ingredients are blended into one. But don't overlook the process. The blender violently combines all separate parts. It uses force, and those parts do not have the power to resist.

As a good leader, you are the force which those you lead cannot resist. You are the master chef working your unselfish magic. You are doing it for them and for the organization. The key is knowing when and when not to apply pressure. As a master chef, you are solely equipped to guide them through this procedure. Each morning I stand in front of my blender knowing the outcome. With each RC, you should know the outcome that you are looking for. As I pour the final product into my glass, there is an expectation and if the expectation is not achieved, it is my fault. When RC arises, you are the

---

[24] Ibid, 6.

one called upon to achieve a favorable end for all parties involved and if not, then you are personally responsible for that.

It is critical to mention that many traditional leaders fall short in this area. Sure, they try to solve the problem, but conflict is not a problem. It is an opportunity. They neither anticipate or envision conflict in this way. They see it as a problem that must be solved. Oftentimes they use harsh tactics to get to the bottom of it and threaten punitive action if it ever occurs again. Recall the two employees I counselled for 6 months; I saw this as an opportunity for them. A chance to get beyond their RC and into a better place, which in turn would make the overall team gel better.

Attempting to avoid conflict and/or addressing it as solely a problem are both counterproductive approaches. These moments of tension will not easily dissipate. Therefore, we must widen the prism through which we understand and relate to conflict. When RC is present, individuals are in competition with each other. They have opposing interests and goals, also known as *competitive outcome interdependence.*[25] The main idea here is competition. When people are in RC, they do not see themselves as coexisting or as a team. They have concluded that they are in a win-lose relationship and they are determined to win. Often this is at the cost of the team and the organization. It can result in a hostile work environment, which is the birth groan of dysfunctional culture.

---

[25] Crasten K.W. De Dreu, "The Virtue and Vice of Workplace Conflict: Food for (Pessimistic) Thought." 7.

On the other hand, you can turn this into a *cooperative outcome interdependence*. The key word here is *cooperative*. Here, when conflicts present themselves, individuals engage in negotiation – open-minded debate that addresses opposing views.[26] This strategy seeks a solution that respects the value of everyone involved and strengthens the team. As an unselfish leader, you are quick to point out that the conflict is normal. You praise them for sharing their individual opinions and stress to them that the best decisions are made when opposing forces come together. You encourage them to listen to each other and find the commonality. You remind them of their shared goals and the benefit that these goals bring to them. If you face and recognize what type of conflict is present and then strategize the proper solution, it will be relatively easy to embrace it.

TRCs can be avoided by ensuring that employees have the proper skills and training to be efficient at their jobs. If the organization has a robust mentoring program, these types of conflicts can be avoided. It is also essential to communicate each team member's role to others in the team. I have witnessed great conflict when either a person does not know her role or others are left in the dark regarding the role of someone on the team. In addition, tension can arise when someone on the team either believes that he can do that specific role better or questions the validity of the person residing in that role. These feelings can lead to RC in the workplace too.

When I was a manager in the manufacturing industry, I took over a position that someone else had previously held. This individual, whom I'll call

---

26 Ibid.

"Tim," was promoted to a different department, but still at the same hierarchical level as I. In other words, he was not my boss. However, Tim felt that he could continue to manage certain members of my team. He would often come into one of my departments when I was not present and talk condescendingly to them. Of course, they complained to me on multiple occasions. Tim was infringing upon the healthy culture we'd created – unity among the group – and he caused the workers to fear him.

After consultation with our boss, I arranged a meeting with Tim. I wanted to understand why he needed to frequent my areas of responsibility and to ensure that we could rectify this situation. He was very agitated, so I started out by sharing with him how valuable he has been to the organization. I thanked him for building the departments I now ran and asked him to allow me to manage these teams according to my style. He made the following statement that still haunts me today. He stated that people are like tools and when one breaks, you simply get another one. I asked him to repeat that… and he did, without batting an eye. I shared with him that I completely disagree; that people have value. Tim responded by saying, "That's your problem. We are in charge and they are here to do what we tell them or they won't do their jobs right." At this point, I perceived that we were not going to get anywhere, so I concluded by reiterating my request that he leave the managing of these departments to me.

I was not satisfied with the outcome of our dialog, so I requested a meeting between him, myself, and our boss. In that second meeting, Tim stated many of the same things he had told me, and our boss was quite disturbed by these sayings. He stressed the damage Tim was causing to our corporate culture and encouraged him to reevaluate his association with the company. Although this got him to back off of my departments, he never changed his view of people. I felt sad for the people who worked directly for me. So TRC can come from many directions, but as an unselfish leader, you must make every effort to mitigate the conflict.

Let's address the conflict that destroys organizations, teams, and individuals. If an organization has "poorly defined jobs, tasks, responsibilities, and authorities,"[27] it will always result in institutional conflict. I've seen people hired with no explanation to the team regarding their roles. I have also seen others promoted and their titles changed without it being communicated to those working alongside them. In both cases, enormous tension ensued. No one knew the person's role, responsibilities, or where their new authority lay. Communication is key when any changes are thought of, let alone implemented. As an unselfish leader, you must clearly define the roles, responsibilities, and authority of everyone on your team.

If you have a "prior history of conflict between two or more people or group,"[28] you have the perfect ingredients for corporate consternation. Recall the two rival employees and their RC which I inherited; I had to quickly address it. By dealing with it head on, I was able to start building a

---

[27] Johnnye L. Morton and Marsha Grace, "Conflict Management and Problem Solving: Leadership Skills for the Reading Professional," *The Reading Teacher* 41, no. 9 (May, 1988): 889.
[28] Ibid.

healthy workplace culture. Long standing animosity can be destructive not only for the individuals involved, but for the staff and customers you serve.

Another potential area of conflict is placing "unreasonable levels of pressure and pace"[29] on your staff. The key word here is *unreasonable*. While we want people to be productive, we must be reasonable about assigning workloads. When it comes to assigning tasks to your staff, it's more about quality deliverables than quantity deliverables. Too much pressure on team members will result in job dissatisfaction and retention problems.

An "overly competitive climate" causes team members to value individual achievements over group success. While one should appreciate a level of competition among group members, it should never lead to a sense of individualism. I often use a basketball analogy to explain the danger of individualism in the workplace. Every player on a basketball team has a specific role to play. If one of them goes solo, defeat is almost guaranteed. Just like in basketball, a soloist will destroy team dynamics and success will be elusive at best.

Collision in the workplace can happen when favoritism is shown to one or more employees. This is a dangerous climate to create. Favoritism empowers the favored over all others. It will break down group unity and trust. It undermines the values of equality and fairness within the team. It creates an atmosphere of fear, bullying, and intimidation. Out of fear, a team

---

[29] Johnnye L. Morton and Marsha Grace, "Conflict Management and Problem Solving: Leadership Skills for the Reading Professional," 889.

member will not speak up to you as a leader or to the favored. Furthermore, when people feel favored among the group, they tend to take short cuts, slack off, and display low levels of commitment. Why? Because they are favored and they know they will not be held accountable. The unfavored is well aware of this non-accountability factor too. Although at times we have to give more attention to one person or another, it must not be seen as showing favoritism. An unselfish leader is the poster child of equality and fairness. There will be situations in which you have a rising star among the team, yet you must not praise him in ways that make others question your motives. Favoritism not only generates conflict; it can lead to questions of unethical behavior in the workplace.

If the organization has a practice of being "punitive, accusative, or threatening,"[30] workers are placed in a highly tensed environment. If mistakes are not viewed as risks worth taken, then people will be afraid to be creative because of punitive action. If accusations easily fly, workers will be emotionally guarded to protect themselves. These negative practices cause team members to retreat into cliques because we need others to support and back us up when we are accused. Another word for threatening is bullying. Have you ever worked in a company where there is an employee that everyone avoids? Maybe the employee has anger issues or is downright rude? To deal with said employee, everyone gives her – her own space; however, in reality, your behavior is being controlled by this employee. In

---

[30] Johnnye L. Morton and Marsha Grace, "Conflict Management and Problem Solving: Leadership Skills for the Reading Professional," 889.

turn, you are being bullied. Silently and indirectly, you are being controlled by the actions of others. No team can begin to operate efficiently under these circumstances.

Too often, many of these conflicts are never addressed. When we consider a company's culture, the practices listed above will destroy it. Unfortunately, people are hired into unhealthy work cultures every day. Unbeknownst to them, an exciting new career opportunity will become their greatest nightmare. This is the reason why we must learn that a job interview is a duo event, meaning the interviewer must also become the interviewee. I offer job interview training and I'm amazed at how many people don't practice this principle. Knowing the correct questions to ask and the proper things to look for can save you years of workplace discomfort and career assassination.

I have learned that honesty is not part of the interview process. I have never been told about the current conflicts in the company at which I was attempting to get a job. This is secret information and unless you know someone on the inside, you will not be aware of these important facts. Yet there are ways to assess how healthy a work culture is. Keep in mind, not every job offer is an opportunity. I should have turned down a lot along the way. During one exit interview, I was asked what did I learn from the job? I simply said, "I learned what not to do as a leader." Of course, my response was not appreciated, but it was an honest one.

How we deal with conflicts in the workplace determines the workplace culture. Later in the book we will examine how to build and maintain a healthy culture environment. Conflict, if handled correctly, can strengthen a team, build trust, and help creativity flourish. If you are among a diverse group of people, conflict will arise. We will never see the world the same or come at every problem alike, but through the work of an unselfish leader, we can strike a balance that benefits everyone involved. The next time you find yourself in a tense situation, don't take it personally. Seeing the world differently is a natural phenomenon within the human species. See this as an opportunity to grow, learn, and become a better you.

What are some of the conflicts you have experienced at work?

_____

_____

_____

_____

_____

_____

_____

What was done to resolve these conflicts?

_____

_____

_____

_____

_____

_____

_____

_____

What were your reactions to the conflicts?

_____

_____

_____

_____

_____

What effects did these conflicts have on the workplace culture?

_____

_____

_____

_____

_____

_____

_____

_____

Chapter 5
Evaluation

I'm about to introduce a controversial way of looking at and conducting an employee evaluation system. It is more of a philosophical approach to evaluating your employees. I am convinced that the current practices related to judging an employee's performance are highly flawed. The current system is rooted in power dynamics and as such is extremely hierarchical. No one looks forward to his annual review, and this must change. When the month of your "annual" approaches, you find yourself dreading the encounter, stressed, and questioning your value. A lot of leaders use this event as an opportunity to reestablish just who is in charge. For that hour or so, they act as if they have your life in their hands and in some regard, they do. I want this system to fundamentally change.

Out in the field, you will encounter some version of the following when it comes to evaluation systems: a numerical marker or some sort of point system designed to indicate whether or not you made the annual grade. Before the review, you will be required to fill out several nonsensical forms relating to your accomplishments over the past year. You might be asked a bunch of stock questions or, in the case of a teacher, you may be observed according to a standardized checklist. None of these methods requires interaction between you and your supervisor. I was once evaluated by a person who saw me a handful of times during meetings. She never observed me doing my job, spent any significant time with me, or interacted with me in a meaningful way, but she evaluated me.

This system used a sort of "Yes, I accomplished this" or "No, I did not" system, so most people found out ahead of time what these performance tasks were and simply tried to do them throughout the year. I might mention that only a few of those items had any correlation to their job descriptions or day-to-day activities. So, imagine this: they received a high rating and got their annual raise, but according to their job descriptions or day-to-day activities, they performed poorly. I can see the practical reasons for using such a system. As a supervisor, you don't have to spend any quality time with employees or interact with them in a substantive way. In this process, all the responsibility is on the employee and all the supervisor has to do is follow the cheat sheet and issue a final grade. Does this sound familiar to you?

As an unselfish leader, you owe it to your team to adequately evaluate them. The evaluation process requires input from you and the employee. It should be a joint effort, so acknowledging this is the initial step to creating a system that works for all. Keep in mind that "attentive guidance and coaching, whether scheduled or spontaneous, should be an ongoing part of your working relationship throughout the year."[31] You cannot evaluate anyone you have not seen or interacted with. For clarity, an annual review is the "process of evaluating the quality of your employees' work and discussing your assessment with them."[32] How can I know the quality of someone's work? Does the basketball coach only show up at the games? Of course not... She is at every practice and every meeting, observing and offering advice and strategies that make an individual player better. By properly

---

[31] Harvard Business Review Press, *Performance Review* (Boston Massachusetts: Harvard Business School Publishing Corporation, 2015), 6.
[32] Ibid, 5.

assessing the skills of one player, the coach knows exactly what the entire team's strengths and weaknesses are.

Who hires a new employee just to watch him fail? Does an NBA franchise waste a valuable draft pick only to see him fail? Of course, not… We bring people into our team because we want them to be successful. Their individual success is the team's success. If they fail, then we as a team are failing ourselves and them. Again, the review should never be a one-sided affair. This joint assessment can be accomplished by consistently engaging and interacting with your employee. The yearly goals should be clear and talked about along the way. Throughout the year, have a sit-down meeting, and document these conversations. Allow the employee to provide written or verbal input regularly, so that there are no surprises at the annual review.

It is critical that an employee feels part of the process. This will build trust and confidence in the fairness of your leadership. No one wants to be evaluated by someone who does not seem to care about her. For a newly hired team member, the first review will establish your relationship moving forward. After her first year, she should feel excited to hear your assessment. And if you have done your job correctly, your review will propel her to greater heights of productivity. However, if you fail at this, you will lose this employee forever. I cannot overstate this scenario. I have seen too many people crushed by their annual review. The supervisor never mentioned any concerns during the year, but dumped it all on at that important hour. How was the unsuspecting staff member supposed to respond? Many are left with the feeling that their job is in jeopardy. The next year they work in fear or look for other employment opportunities. What a waste.

In the last chapter I explored the impact of showing favoritism in the workplace. Well, favoritism can rear its ugly head here too. Very likely, you have seen it yourself in full effect: the employee that is close to the boss. Laughs at every joke. Rushes to get the boss a cup of coffee. The tattletale on everyone except himself. If you have not witnessed this, you are one of the lucky ones. Everyone knows this person has become untouchable because the boss favors him. I found out one time that our boss had requested an employee to keep a log on one of the team members. Of course, this was unbeknownst to said team member. It was discovered by a third team member when the spy forgot to close out the log on a shared computer. You can imagine the panic that went through the entire staff. Trust was already at an all-time low, but now, trust was completely shattered. Everyone knew this clandestine spy was the manager's favorite and, therefore, untouchable. The manager consulted this log during this employee's annual review. Shameful…

No evaluation system will work if favoritism is involved. Team members will not trust your assessment or you. In cases like these, employees are simply working in survival mode. It's worth mentioning the challenges that one faces when the ego comes into play as a leader. The human desire is to receive affirmation and acceptance. These two actions spark a certain feeling within us all, yet they can be quite deceptive. In other words, the ego feeds off of flattery. An unselfish leader must be disciplined in all situations. From time to time, you will have an employee that deploys this methodology and you must not fall for it. How much does the ego control your life? Be careful! This is not a deviation from our topic.

If we are going to evaluate employees properly, we must view them all the same. It might be necessary for you to correct the behavior of a team member when it comes to flattery. It is not appropriate and it will lead to you extending favoritism toward this individual. You may never set out for it to happen, but without being sensitive to your ego, you could easily fall into this downward spiral. I have seen the effects of this first-hand in several organizations. It speaks more to the fragility of the leader than to the perpetrator. The ego desires gratification and adoration. It is the biggest flaw that a traditional leader possesses. Remember, we are the greatest servant among our team; we must be beyond blemish.

How do you gather proper information for the evaluation? This requires time and patience. You cannot accomplish this overnight. Too many traditional leaders try to make this a drive-thru experience; they try to gather all the information the week of the evaluation. Gathering information is an ongoing procedure. Listen, an unselfish leader knows her people, their families, their desires in life, and where they are heading. You are personally involved and intimately involved in their lives, and they know it. It's the smallest of conversations and interactions that matter. You gather information about their past, their struggles, and their aspirations. In other words, you have them convinced that you care. This job of caring is not to placate them. You have a genuine concern for their life and stability.

What statements do they make? What concerns do they have? What contributions have they made? How do they interact with others? What causes them stress and how do they handle it? These are only a few questions to observe when you are making note of them.

As mentioned earlier, you should be interacting with your employee throughout the evaluation process. Yes, the evaluation process is a year-long endeavor. Document these observations and the consistent conversations throughout the year, so at the annual performance evaluation, you have the paperwork to reassure the employee that you have been paying attention. The meeting tone is very important. Don't do the assessment sitting behind your desk. Your desk represents a demarcation and places the worker in an inferior position. I recommend an open space, not a table. Just two chairs to symbolize equality and respect. Take a moment to stress that this is an extension of the ongoing conversations and interactions you have had throughout the year.

Such an approach will place the employee at ease and set the stage for a positive outcome. Begin by asking the employee his impressions of goals and accomplishments of the prior year. Remember, your employees are part of the evaluation process. I must stress that this is not the time for negative feedback. You should have supplied that at the appropriate time. You should offer only constructive criticism. Constructive criticism can be easily digested between two positive statements such as, "You did an awesome job on improving the procurement process. I thought others should have been included sooner, but the end result was amazing." You just acknowledged the get job he did, but you advised him to include more of the team, earlier on.

I want to offer a new philosophy for evaluating people. The philosophy begins with you. You need to exercise empathy for the employee. In other words, you must place yourself in her position. She has worked for you all year and she is a valuable member of your team. You have the responsibility of ensuring that she has the resources to do her job, and that the culture in which the work is done is a healthy one. You must also consider that she should be treated with respect and dignity even when she makes mistakes. You acknowledge your flaws, limitations, and deficiencies. If you can arrive at these philosophical points, then you are capable of looking at the employee in a holistic way.

Next, evaluate your commitment throughout the year when it came to your responsibilities regarding the evaluation. Did you spend time with the employee, and how valuable was that time? Did you observe and document his performance? Did you offer constructive criticism when needed? How much positive feedback did you offer throughout the year? These are critical questions to ask yourself and to take a moment to answer on paper.

Did you spend time with the employee? How valuable was that time?

_____

_____

_____

_____

_____

Did you observe and document the employee's performance? Briefly describe it.

_____

_____

_____

_____

_____

_____

What constructive criticism did you offer?

_____

_____

_____

_____

What positive feedback did you provide throughout the year?

_____

_____

_____

_____

If you are an employee seeking to be in leadership one day, it is important that you answer these questions of your current supervisor. Do you feel that he contemplated these things about you? Remember, we learn from an incompetent leader as much as a competent one. Some of the best examples of what a good leader should do can be found through observation of poor leadership. It's called the opposite effect or learning what not to do. Although these are painful experiences, without pain, how would we know joy? And without sorrow, how would we know happiness? It's the opposite effect.

Now, as an unselfish leader, you have easily answered the aforementioned questions, so you are ready to turn your attention outward. Show excitement for the upcoming review with your employee. I usually tell them how much I'm looking forward to having the evaluation conversation with them. Yes, it is a conversation. It gives you an opportunity to praise the employee for their yearly efforts. The outcome is not only a reflection of them, but how well you have led them.

During the conversation, avoid all disruptions. This moment is the most important time you will have with them. Be on your best behavior, so put down your cell phone and do not answer your office line. Have everything prepared and organized before they arrive. There is nothing more deflating then having your supervisor search through a cluttered desk looking for your evaluation. Start out by asking them their observations over the course of the past year. I'm sure that if you have observed and interacted with them, your documentation will reflect some of these observations. This let the team member know just how well you have been paying attention.

Then, it's your opportunity to share your thoughts. Remember, no surprises… As an unselfish leader, you are practicing empathy, so you envision yourself sitting across from yourself. What would you want to hear? How would you feel about hearing a destructive criticism? I think we all know the answer to that. After you have reinforced some of their observations, give in detail your findings. Watch careful for their body language. Never forget, this is an encouraging conversation. After you are finish, ask the employee for feedback. Address every issue they bring up and if necessary, give solutions.

At this point, reflect on last year's goals. Thank them for accomplishing the agreed upon goals and move onto setting new yearly goals. Be sure to make the goals realistic and obtainable. Lastly, discuss merit increases, even if the company is currently under a pay freeze. You can offer other incentives like gift cards, or team building incentives, a book, etc. Don't let them walk out empty handed. Yes, I am asking you to invest some of your hard-earned money into your team. Teachers routinely buy supplies to benefit their students and they have some of the lowest salaries in our country. The benefits of such a gesture will outweigh any financial loss you might feel. It shows them that you truly care. I guarantee this employee will walk out of your office feeling ten feet tall and highly encouraged.

Now, this chapter would be incomplete without addressing an unflattering evaluation. From time to time, you will find yourself in this situation. You must ask yourself the following questions: How did we get here? Have I done everything possible to redeem this employee? Do I have the proper paperwork to validate a suspect evaluation? Have I addressed and documented throughout the year the employee's shortcomings? After being at a job for two months, I was asked to conduct a yearly appraisal on an employee that my supervisor was not pleased with. I shared with my supervisor that I was not comfortable doing this. I had not observed this person long enough or built a relationship with him. My supervisor insisted that I was in charge and it was my responsibility.

Of course, I was not pleased with this feedback and again reiterated by displeasure, yet she ordered me to. Therefore, I explained the situation to the employee, gave him a neutral (average) evaluation, set goals, and promised him that he would have every opportunity to excel. This team member ended up being a star and well respected in the workplace. Needless to say, I gained no favor with my supervisor. However, it was the right thing to do.

If you have done everything within your power, then you have to be open and honest with the employee. Show them the documented conversations, observations, and suggestions for improving throughout the year. While the review is painful for them, offer them a new start. I often say to them that I have just hired them and this is their first day on the job. Let's start fresh… Let's throw away what we think we know about each other and begin a new relationship. I encourage you to set small obtainable goals with them. Ones that can be achieved in a short amount of time. This will give them a sense of accomplishment and you an opportunity to praise them for their newfound effort. It is also a good idea to give them a book on what you know their challenges to be.

Traditionally evaluating people is outdated and many of the new platforms are built upon this archaic thinking. We must think about and approach this differently and innovatively. I have shared with you an approach that is failproof. It requires your participation, but the outcome is a win-win. Take a few moments and write down how you can implement this new philosophy:

_____

_____

_____

_____

_____

_____

_____

_____

_____

Chapter 6
Buffer

In the last chapter, I illustrated a situation in which I was put between an employee and my supervisor. Being placed in this awkward position is what I call buffering. A lot of a leader's time is spent acting as a buffer. A buffer is defined "as a person or thing that prevents incompatible or antagonistic people or things from coming into contact with or harming each other."[33] Looking back at that supervisor, she had a score that she wanted to use me to settle with that employee. It's sad, but too many people simply carry out the hedonistic passions of those from whom they take orders. Remember: you are an unselfish leader, so it is not about you or what you might lose. Oftentimes we are called to stand in the gap between two opposing forces. Whether it is upper management or a next level supervisor, you are positioned to prevent incompatible or antagonistic people or things from hurting those you have been entrusted to lead.

At times this can be a very lonely place to reside. It requires a strong sense of self, and one must not be too sensitive to criticism. Continuing with the same example, my supervisor saw this as betrayal, and our relationship never recovered. She wanted me to carry out her dirty work, and my refusal to do so put me in a position of isolation. Recall, I had only been there for a couple of months. I ended up staying on for 6 years, yet she was never kind or supportive. I could write several pages of analysis so you could understand why someone would place a newly hired manager in this position, but it would be a waste of our time.

---

[33] Dictionary.com, s.v., "citation," accessed March 24, 2019, https://www.dictionary.com/browse/buffer?s=t.

Have you ever received a call from your boss in which he asked you to look into a concern about one of your team members? If so, you have just entered the buffer zone. I recall a time in the Navy involving a team member whom I supervised. I'll call him "Pete." Pete was actually senior to me and, in fact, was close to retirement. He made a maintenance mistake that caused damage to some equipment. Of course, my boss was extremely upset, and he requested that I discipline Pete. Under my authority this was Pete's only mistake, so I tried to plead with my supervisor for mercy on his behalf. He was just 2 years from laying down his anchors. My boss wanted to give him the ultimate punishment that could be given to someone close to retirement: he wanted to demote him a rank, therefore reducing the pension Pete had spent 18 years acquiring.

I argued that we should instead show leniency with Pete's consequence: restrict him to the ship, give him extra duty, and remove him from his current position. But my supervisor wanted blood. As you can imagine, Pete was fearful of what the outcome might be. I spent a lot of time trying to prepare him for this finality. As a buffer, I was pleading for someone and attempting to bring comfort to him. When that unfortunate day arrived, my boss did exactly what he set out to do. And afterward, I watched – for two years – as that guy walked around with one less chevron on his sleeve, until he retired at one rank lower than he should have. I still think about that today. How could I have been a better buffer for him?

You rarely find yourself being a buffer when good news is part of the equation. Traditional supervisors rarely want you to be the bearer of good news. That duty feeds their egos too much to hand over the privilege to you. It's the bad news they need to hide from – difficult changes to the organization and the like – so this is where you come in. In other words, buffering is costly. It can be costly to you personally and to those you are trying to protect. If you are not a principled person, you will find it hard to be a buffer. If you are worried about your career, how people view you, or what you might lose by doing the right thing, then you can and will never enter the buffer zone. You will simply end up doing the bidding of those over you.

From time to time, management will have burdensome changes that need to be implemented, and it is your job to convey this in a way that does not devastate your team. Normally these changes are bluntly communicated to you and other managers. Conventional wisdom says that you are supervisors, and therefore you can be straight up and direct. Again, we need unselfish leaders at every level of management. Being a supervisor does not shield you from feeling defeated when egregious changes are introduced. I hope that among those discussing this change information are at least a few unselfish leaders: leaders who are not willing simply to head to their team and relay the message, and then wait for someone to complain so they can take names and walk away.

An unselfish leader will internalize the information before articulating the information to those affected. This type of leader will measure his words and fully analyze the impact of them. How will this affect our culture? If it is layoffs, how can I help prepare my team for this? When I was a manager in the manufacturing industry, I learned that our facility was going to closed down. This information was conveyed to me just a few days before the

Thanksgiving holiday when the Vice President of Operations flew in from headquarters. He called the plant together and delivered the bad news to everyone. Later on that day, he offered a turkey to anybody who might want one.

I recall my one-on-one conversation with this VP, and I remember his telling me that the news "hurts me more than you can imagine." It was a funny statement – he still had his job and a secured position. I, on the other hand, had just built my first home. My first thought was, how can I tell my wife that in about a month I will be jobless? And when it came to being the buffer, well, my supervisor was robbed of the opportunity to be one for us. He was an unselfish leader and I know he would have prepared us for the news. In addition, the VP's conversation was all about what the company needed to do. They needed to consolidate and we had been chosen for closure. He said that for months they had been losing money, and our center was a debt center – meaning, we were never designed to make money. So, given these circumstances, how could we help the company in its troubles? Up until that point, no one even knew that was our status.

I would find out in the coming days that my boss had fought to keep me on board, so the company offered me a job at the headquarters. My boss did exactly what an unselfish leader should do. He was working earnestly to help all of us with the transition. While I truly appreciated his efforts, I was not willing to leave the state and had to decline. Just three years earlier I had departed the Navy and my parents were getting up in age; the distance would have been too much for me to bear. But my boss advocating for a new position is exactly how you buffer. The person buffering does not have to inform the recipients of his efforts on their behalf. As a buffer, you often operate in the shadows and share only when you have it figured out or you have reached a conclusion. There is no need to offer hope, or to usher in despair, until you know the final outcome.

There are also occasions in which you are called on to be a buffer by a team member. You might be asked to find out a bit of information or to sense the mood toward a necessary request before that person goes forward with it. It sounds like a kind of espionage mission. Who doesn't like a good adventure? I know I do. So, in this instance, being a buffer can be extremely covert. If you are ever asked in this matter, you can believe that the requester trusts you. Take comfort in knowing you have gained this level of trust. In the workplace, just like life, trust is easily given, easily lost, and even more difficult to recapture when broken. In the chapter on team building, we will deeply examine trust, so for now, it is enough to recognize that trust is one of the most fragile aspects of the human experience.

Being a buffer requires a unique perspective of your relationship to the company versus your team. I mean that when you are hired, you are brought on board to fulfill the company's mission. The company pays you, provides you benefits, and requires a level of loyalty. To complicated matters, your team is in the same position, yet you have a vested interest in the lives of those you lead. How can I be true to the company's mission and maintain a sense of loyalty, while honoring my obligation as a leader? I'm so glad you asked.

An unselfish leader can only be true and loyal to that which is right for everyone involved. After all, whether it is upper management or among the lowest ranks, humanity is the common denominator. You must consider everyone who is affected by your decisions, and when you make your decision you must be willing to articulate and stand by it. You must seek the truth and what is most honorable when you are buffering. Shouldn't your principles define this for you? What are your principles? Do you believe in equality, dignity, and self-respect for all? Do you reject a hierarchical formula that places people in favor over others? Does your lowest paid employee have the same value as the CEO? Would you do as I have done in not punishing an employee with a bad evaluation given those circumstances I mentioned earlier?

When you buffer, you operate with integrity. You don't forfeit this for personal gain or to maintain your status in the eyes of others. As a buffer, sometimes you might have to take the fall. You might have to lose favor for doing the right thing. This is the job of a good leader. Throughout my career, I have had to pay the price for buffering, yet I would have had it no other way. In the end, those who questioned you will ultimately respect you. We are loyal to empowering others and improving the human condition. When you refuse to buffer, you may win the battle, but the war will be lost. You may please your boss, but you will hurt others. Not just that individual, but his family as well. Whether it is a loss of pay, job, or a loss of dignity, this carries outside of the workplace. Who would want to be responsible for the destruction of a life? Not an unselfish leader. She is a builder and giver of life to those she is entrusted to care for. Do not underestimate the power you have been given.

If you buffer correctly and strategically, you will protect the organization and its employees. Buffering is not a zero-sum game. Going back to the illustration of egregious changes announced, one could handle it this way. Let's say there's a company layoff coming in two months. You gather your team, share the specifics for such a drastic change, and ensure them that you will do everything in your power to assist them in finding new jobs. Let them know this is the beginning of our discussions and they are not alone in working this out. Let them know that everyone on this team is valuable and if we lose anyone, it will be a very sad day, but like so many things in life, we will uncover a way to pick up the pieces and move on. In addition, tell everyone that as soon as you know something you will convey the news to them, and guarantee them that whatever you know, they will know. Finally, tell them you will be meeting with them individually to discuss this further and to look at ways to help. This is exactly what a buffer and an unselfish leader does.

What else could you do as a buffer and unselfish leader?

_____

_____

_____

_____

_____

_____

Where have you seen buffering in full effect? Has your supervisor been an example of this for you, or have you been a buffer for someone? Describe in detail…

_____

_____

_____

_____

_____

_____

_____

_____

I have always viewed myself as a caretaker of these faithful souls and the organization, and of my vision of the work we do. You are a mentor, you are a champion for diversity, you create a culture in which they coexist, you approach conflict head on and see it as an opportunity for growth, you are a trusted evaluator, and now you are a buffer. Wear these titles with honor and accept the challenges that each one brings. You are on your way to being an unselfish leader.

Scenario: *Buffering*

You're the new manager and you have been hired to lead a small staff. These staff members have been in conflict for a long time, and your boss has a reputation for firing all of your predecessors. Of course, you find this out only after accepting the new position. Your new boss has it in for one of your staff members. It becomes clear that he wants you to have an unfavorable view of this employee and he outright tells you that you should get rid of her. The only problem is that you find this employee to be competent, reliable, humble, and good at her job. After about 6 months, you are called upon to conduct this employee's evaluation. Now, you are fully aware that your boss is expecting you to nail her to the wall; however, your intention is quite the opposite. You want to reward her because she has been one of your best employees.

How do you handle this situation?

_____

_____

_____

_____

_____

_____

_____

When you are buffering, it is not always a comfortable position to be in. However, it is a necessary one for the protection and empowerment of those you lead. Take this responsibility seriously and stand up for those who do not have the power to stand up for themselves.

"Ultimately, leadership is not about glorious crowning acts. It's about keeping your team focused on a goal and motivated to do their best to achieve it, especially when the stakes are high and the consequences really matter. It is about laying the groundwork for others' success, and then standing back and letting them shine."- Chris Hadfield

Chapter 7
Decision-Making

How do you make decisions? This is a critical question to answer. Too many times decisions are made either in isolation or absent of important information. I know you've heard that decisions have consequences, and yes, they do. A correct decision can be celebrated by all, but a poor one can be costly to everyone involved. Your team is dependent on you to make decisions that are right and beneficial to them. No decision should be made to benefit the leader. Decisions that benefit the leader are more common than I would like to acknowledge. Some decisions are made simply to save face for the supervisor or to please higher-ups. Others are made without considerations of the impact on the ones we are called to lead.

When a decision is made to benefit only the person in charge, the team culture and team dynamics suffer. I must preface the above statement by adding that it will suffer if other voices have not been included in the decision being made. A practice like this indicates that the culture and dynamics are already on shaky ground. I don't want to get ahead of myself. In the chapter on Organizational and Team Culture we will discuss in detail culture and dynamics; for the moment, the crucial point is that everyone should have a voice, whether direct or implicit, in the very decisions that affect them.

Allowing others an implicit voice means you know your team and how they respond in certain situations so well that this knowledge influences how you make decisions. In such instances, after the decision is made, you as the leader explain this rationale to them. Keep in mind that every decision falls into the two categories: positive and negative. And the same decision can be viewed by team members differently. For instance, the decision to offer overtime to your employees can be viewed positively by those looking to make more money, or negatively for the worker who is also a parent needing to pick up his kids right after normal working hours. An unselfish leader knows his staff and approaches decision making with empathy, anticipating the potential positive and negative impacts. In the above scenario, one might say, "Production is behind and we have been authorized to work overtime, yet I know this may cause problems for those who have children in school. Therefore, I want to meet with each of you individually to discuss any negative impact this could have on you, and ways we can minimize that."

Oftentimes, employees feel like they have no choice but to comply when corporate decisions are made without their input, so they remain quiet and suffer in silence. Think about the mother or father hearing this news and wondering how will their child get home from school? Imagine if they have to be there when the bus arrives dropping their son or daughter home. Will they continue to be a productive part of your team? Now, there are many people in leadership positions that feel you must fall in line. You have no choice, if you want to keep your job. This is why possessing empathy for others is so important. Being able to place yourself in the position of those you lead is one of the most needed qualities in a leader.

From my work experiences, the majority of people in leadership positions do not exhibit empathy towards others. While requiring everyone to work overtime will please the higher-ups, it could cause someone to lose their job. Without considering the impact on certain staff members, the supervisor has complied with a decision that only benefits him or his superiors. In other words, he is managing up. His concern is only for pleasing those to whom he is accountable and not those under his stewardship. This is not leadership. It is a dictatorship.

I have shown you how a simple decision can be life altering for a staff member when he is not included either directly or implicitly. As a leader, how many decisions do you make every day? In actuality, one does not have to be a supervisor to affect the lives of others through daily decisions. How seriously do we take the decision we have to make today? Have you ever worked for someone who never considers the impact of his decisions on your life? I know I have. It was one of the most horrendous situations I had ever been in. He made impulsive and oftentimes explosive decisions daily. The type of decisions that increase workplace pressures and anxiety. The kind of decisions that require counseling for PTSD. He was impervious to the harm and torture he was causing those under his sociopathic leadership.

I hope that you have never had to endure that. However, I hope you are not reading this and the person I described above is the same person you see when you look in the mirror. Many so-called leaders wake up to seeing this person in their mirror every day. Yet, because of their ego, fragility, insensitivity, carelessness, sociopathy, and narcissism, they are blind to who they really are. They have no idea of how others view them simply because a servant will never question a dictator. They will just kowtow out of fear of retribution or being fired. Sadder yet, many so-called leaders thrive on creating this atmosphere of fear. They make decisions knowing they will wreak havoc in the lives of their staff. As a matter of fact, this is their leadership style. A style of fear and intimidation by using their decision-making as the preferred rod of punishment.

I recall an incident in the Navy. I had a supervisor who decided that every day we would work late. Granted, we had just gotten off a six-month deployment. But I had a young son at home, and the work was not there to warrant extended hours. He stated that his wife walked out on him while we were deployed, so he had nothing to go home to, and therefore, why should we be allowed to go home? Of course, I had a sound answer to his rhetorical question, but he was having none of it. Day after day, 5 pm, 6 pm, 7 pm would pass as we all sat talking in the engineering room. He didn't care that we had nothing to do. He simply wanted us to suffer because he was in pain. This is the key…

The key reason "position" authority leaders will inflict pain: they themselves are in pain. The façade is easy to recognize if you know the symptoms. I already listed some above. They have a huge, fragile ego. Instability is their best friend, and they are married to anger. When their decisions are questioned, they threaten and then act passively aggressively towards you. This Navy supervisor was a poster child for irrationality and for the type who thrives on creating his own chaos. As unselfish leaders, we seek harmony and peace in all the decisions we make. While everyone has a certain amount of heartache, we are wise not to cast that on others. While I truly despised being subjected to such unwarranted and undeserving misery, I learned a lot from it. I learned how not to treat those I lead. Fortunately, I had many unselfish supervisors in the Navy that modelled the best examples of what a leader should be.

The best decision-making process includes voices of those most affected by the decision. How do you include those affected? First, recognize that corporate / team decisions are the most productive. They send a message that all voices matter. They empower, and they provide an opportunity for sharing ownership in the decision made. Secondly, the majority wins. You must not invite all voices and then go against the majority of those voices. This is hypocritical and squanders trust. I had just joined a company as a high-level director when the staff was having a heated but productive debate over an important decision. The supervisor of the company shared her displeasure with the overall majority of the staff's decision, but agreed that she would stand with it. The big meeting in which the decision would be announced was the following day. Some of the most powerful members of the community gathered at the meeting and the supervisor addressed those in attendance. She outlined the controversy and stated how difficult a decision this was for everyone involved. But her next words hit the staff like a lightning rod. She went on to say that the staff agreed that "Mr. Jones" should be awarded the contract. Much to my and others' dismay, the staff had not come to that conclusion. They'd agreed that he should not receive it. Needless to say, however, Mr. Jones was given the contract.

As I looked around the room, I could see the betrayal on the faces of staff members. They were angered and felt devalued and deceived. From my perspective, they were completely duped. The next day several came into my office and vented their anger. They asked me how could she do this and how can we trust her again? These are valid and important questions that must be answered if there is a chance of rebuilding trust. They asked me for advice. I suggested that they go to her, express their discomfort with the decision, and give her an opportunity to explain. But at that point, they did not trust who they were being led by. Would she listen or would she fire them for their opposition? I felt very concerned for them and for myself. I had just come on board. I suggested that we address this at tomorrow's staff meeting.

At the staff meeting, you could feel the tension in the air. The meeting began in the usual manner. People reported on their various areas of expertise. At this point, I sensed that the supervisor had no desire to address the events of yesterday. A young staff member couldn't help himself and he launched right in. "Why did you go against staff recommendations?" The supervisor was quick to reply, "I'm in charge here, and I don't have to explain myself to you." OUCH!!! Of course, I was having the same thoughts this young staff member was expressing, and my next thought was, "What have I gotten myself into?" This quick exchange between the two of them sent a chill through the rest of the staff. I felt bad for the young man. He had the courage to speak up, and no one was willing to support him. I know they were feeling the same way because they told me so. I could not leave him out there by himself, so I piped in.

"Well," I said to the supervisor, "no one here is questioning who is in charge. Additionally, we know that you have to make some hard decisions that we don't have all the information regarding. Furthermore, you are under a lot of pressure, and we want to support you as best as we can. However, we left the room with a corporate, agreed-upon decision, and you went in a different direction, so I think we are entitled to the reasons behind your change of mind." Silence fell in the conference room. I can only imagine the thoughts going through her mind. It would be completely counterproductive to disregard the guy you just hired. I realized at that moment I had seen her style before, and it scared me. She was fragile and felt that questioning her was an act of disloyalty. I think I sealed my fate that day.

After pausing, she stated "You are right; I guess you deserve an explanation." (*I guess?!*) She went on. "There are things that I cannot share with you and you just have to trust me. It had to go that way." Oh no. Not the "you just have to trust me" philosophy. Who blindly trusts anyone? Over time, trust is earned, nurtured, and proven to be reliable. Ma'am, I don't even know you. Well, that's how the conversation concluded and, in the end, she fired my young coworker. She strategized over several months to accomplish this feat. She was not a leader. She was a dictator. Needless to say, I lasted no more than about five years with this company, as the leadership was more of the same – selfish and non-empathic.

As an unselfish leader, you stand with the staff. If you lead them, please don't deceive them. When you include their voices, they must carry the same weight as yours. Let your yes be yes and your no be no. Please don't be unstable and waver when the pressure is on you.

It's necessary to say a little about the supporting cast who did not support that young man even though they felt the same way. If you are in this situation, never let a teammate stand alone. It's selfish and disloyal. That young man had the courage to speak for us all, and he deserved our reinforcement. I know this can be and often is costly to one's bottom line, yet it is the right thing to do. If we don't do what is right, who will?

The above situation illustrates the complexities of upper-management decision making versus middle-management decision making. Obviously, the supervisor got a lot of pressure from her board to go a different direction. If you are a high-level executive, as was the supervisor in this case, you cannot do what is best for a select few. The impact of your decision cannot be taken that lightly. Just recently, I heard about rapid turnover at that organization. How can an unstable corporation ever reach their mission and goals? In the final analysis, this causes more harm than good. You find yourself constantly rebuilding and repeating the process of trying to create a healthy culture in which people feel valued and look forward to coming to work.

It is critical to be aware that our decisions have lasting impacts. We must move beyond this primal thinking about decisions as only having consequences on the person making them. We are only part of the process. We must be part of a process that ensures a win-win situation. It's shortsighted to assume that everyone will immediately fall in line. People need to process and arrive at their own conclusion about what does or does not complicate their lives. Implicitly, we can control some of this, if we know those we lead. We know their families, their aspirations, goals, and challenges. We must consider all of the known factors while coming to our own conclusions. Be a leader to those you are accountable to and be a leader to those you uplift every day. While you are ultimately responsible, the buck does not stop with you. As an unselfish leader, I want my people involved and I want them to feel that their voices matter. They matter in the good and bad decisions we agree upon. We are in this decision-making process together. We succeed or fail together…

How do you make your decisions?

_____

_____

_____

_____

_____

_____

Explain a difficult decision you have made.

_____

_____

_____

_____

How do you include others in the decisions that need to be made?

_____

_____

_____

_____

_____

"The secret to success is good leadership, and good leadership is all about making the lives of your team members or workers better."-
Tony Dungy

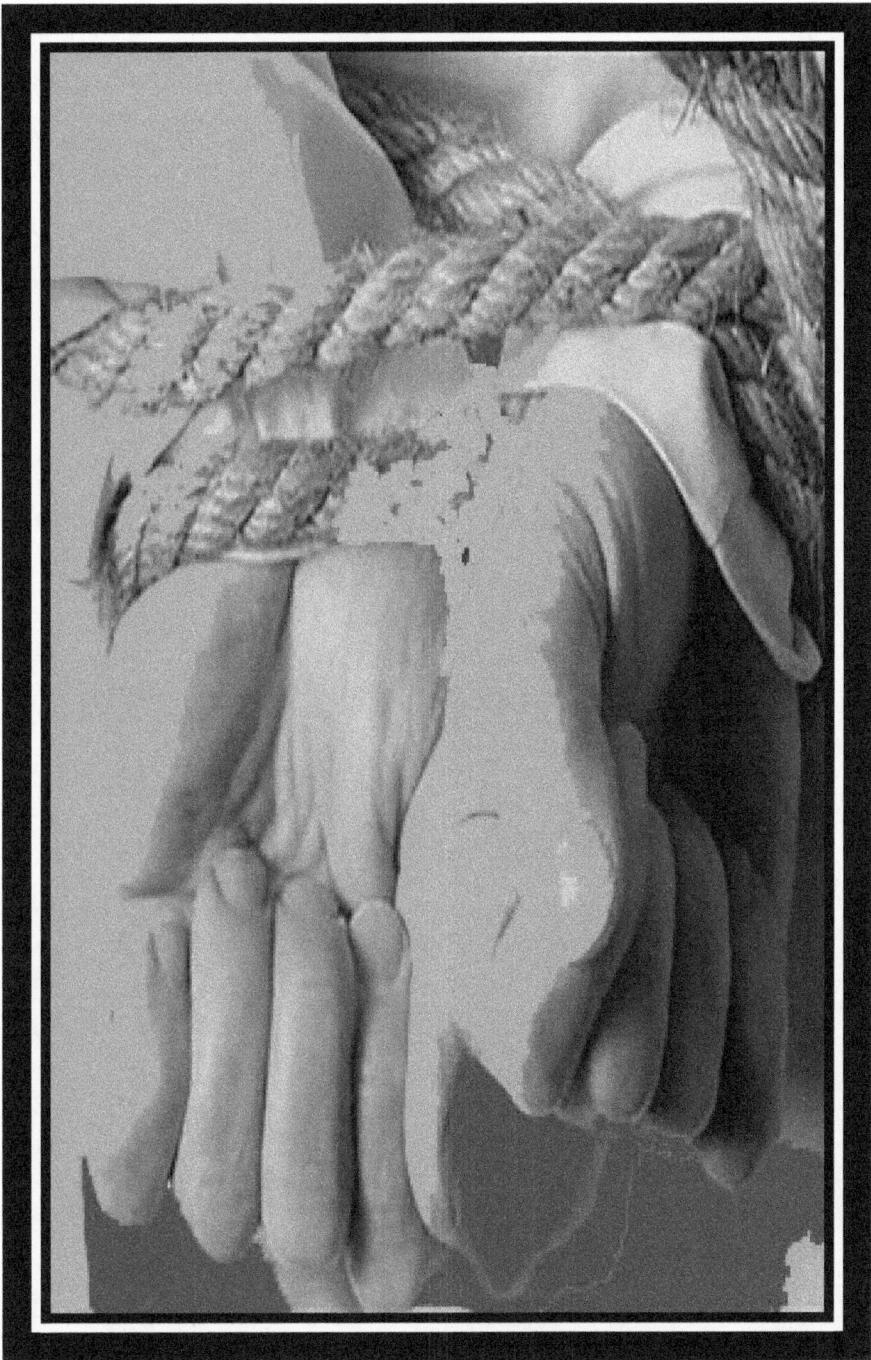

Chapter 8
Total Control

I've tossed in this chapter because there is a growing tendency among leaders to control every aspect of the persons working for them. The proper term here is micromanaging. Undoubtedly, you have encountered one or more micromanagers in your professional career. What is this need to control others? Some leaders mask this as some need to be involved in every aspect of the company. They hide behind the notion of caring so much that they want to help you with your day-to-day responsibilities. Oftentimes they can come across as being very supportive. They undoubtedly know the core language to use, such as "We support each other around here" or the classic, "You don't work for me, we work together." Of course, comments like these are designed to soften you up for the blow to come. Others are not so covert. They will tell you that their way of thinking and doing the job is the only way it should be done. Yes, I have actually heard that said.

Micromanagers are highly manipulative and volatile. If they cannot manipulate you, they feel like they are losing control. They thrive on control and being in charge. They only exist to con you into thinking they are superior and you are better off following every detail they give you. They are not interested in your thoughts, talents, creativity, or expertise for, in their eyes, you have none of those. They hired you to control you for their own agenda. I'm not being an alarmist when I suggest that they are inherently sociopaths and/or narcissists. Unfortunately, they are… They will gaslight you at every turn and lie without ceasing. They will ultimately, I think, come to believe every lie they tell. This is not a pretty characterization of anyone, but so many of this type occupy leadership positions.

These people are so good at manipulation that unless you are in a relationship with one or work for one, no one outside views them this way. Remember, they are so savvy at masking how horrible they can be that if you complain or tell others about their behavior, you won't be believed. Because of these traits, being a supervisor, manager, or director are positions they seek out. Every aspect of their person is masterly deceptive, and they have spent years perfecting these grotesques qualities.

They are volatile because they are so wrapped up in their own self-gratification that they don't have the capacity to feel the pain they are inflicting on you. Their explosive behavior detonates every time you disagree with them. They are volatile because there is no balance to them. The weight of every relationship must tilt in their favor. If not, they will aggressively fight to bring the pendulum back to their side. If you call them out or catch them in a lie with no escape, they will say something like, "I'm sorry if I hurt you." Notice, the *if* I hurt you. I once told a micromanaging boss straight out that he had offended me with his comments. His immediate reply was, "I'm sorry if I offended you." I replied, "I just told you that you have offended me." He went on to ask, "How would you like to deal with this?" So – get this – *he* offends *me*, and *I* have to decide how [*he*] should deal with it? Micromanagers will always place the responsibility on you. Even when they make the mistake and make all the decisions, they will find a way to make it your fault, and therefore, your responsibility. They hate being held accountable.

The verb form of control means "to exercise restraint or direction over; dominate; command."[34] A fitting depiction of a controller is someone who seeks to dominate and break you down. He knows that if your self-esteem can be destroyed, he has you right where he wants you. Micromanagers dominate by overwhelming you and constantly pushing you further away from your true self. They work to get you to the point at which you question your abilities and even your sanity. While it's hard not to take this personally, you should try not to. They treat everyone this way. It's all about them and what they desire. The sociopath in them has no conscience or ability to show empathy. In a strange way, it's not their fault. They were socialized this way. Experts believe that something traumatic happened in their childhood that has rendered them incapable of behaving with decency towards another person.

Let's look at the traits of a micromanager:

1. Resists delegating work
2. Inserts and immerses herself in the work assigned to others
3. Looks at the detail instead of the big picture
4. Discourages others from making decisions
5. Gets involved in the work of others without consulting them
6. Monitors what's least important and expects regular reports on miscellany
7. Pushes aside the experience and knowledge of colleagues
8. Loose loyalty and commitment
9. Focuses on the wrong priorities

---

[34] Dictionary.com, s.v., "citation," accessed April 9, 2019, https://www.dictionary.com/browse/control?s=t.

10. Has a demotivated team[35]

Yeah, some of you have known someone like this, I'm sure. They hired you to do a job, yet they never let you do it. I once worked for a firm that hired me for a new position. I was asked to write the job description, which I did. Although I wrote the job description, my supervisor felt the need to tell me how to do the job. He wanted to meet with me on every task I attempted, and went as far as to tell me how I should do it. It became clear that he hired me to do only and precisely what he wanted me to do. When I tried to be creative, he told me he didn't agree with my ideas and forced me to do it his way. He was a classic example of a selfish leader. It was all about him.

Although they will minimize you in every area of your job, they will yet steal from you. I noticed that this supervisor would write down all my suggestions. He also asked me to give him names of key people I knew and have had relationships with. One time he noticed on my calendar that I had a meeting with a prominent leader and he told me that he should have been in that meeting as well. I asked him why should you have been? He stated that with all the important people I meet with, he needs to be invited. After a while it occurred to me that he was stealing my ideas, and he was trying to profit off of the relationships I'd spent years establishing. He hired me to control and use me.

---

[35] Martin Webster and Vicky Webster, "10 Signs of Micromanagement — Strategies for Dealing With Micromanagers," Leadership Thoughts, https://www.leadershipthoughts.com/10-signs-of-micromanagement/

In the previous chapter, we talked about how important it is to have others involved in the decision-making process. A micromanager will discourage such an effort. Remember that they are always trying to control you and every situation. If you have a part in making a decision, then they have given up control. Again, this is their greatest fear – losing control. An unselfish leader shares control. She wants your buy-in and your ownership of the process. For an unselfish leader, it's not about an individual. It is about the collective voice and the diversity of input everyone brings.

Micromanagers will discount your experience and knowledge. They say things like, "I know you don't understand this," or "I know this is all new to you." It's laughable because they never ask if you understand or have seen it before. By letting you bring your experiences and knowledge into the workplace, they risk the chance of others seeing you as capable. Remember, he is the only one that is capable. He has built a career on manipulating people into believing he must be consulted on every detail.

Why did you hire me? That is an essential question one silently asks when under the direction of a micromanager. For during the interview process, they sell you on the idea of inclusion and will even tell others how thankful they are to have you on the team. All the while, their only desire is to control you like they do to the rest of the staff. You've walked into a culture of fear and compliance. Unbeknownst to you, they have seen a weakness in you. You are kind and understanding, and represent a purity that they can corrupt. It sounds quite devious – and it is. If you are unfortunate enough to find yourself in this situation, what do you do? I'm glad you asked that question. You get out.

Being under this type of leadership kills the soul. You will not win. You will not change this person or change the organizational culture. The only decision you need to make is when to resign. If you are in this situation, begin to develop an exit plan. Update your resume, avoid this person at all cost, seek counseling, and remember that you matter. You are the same person as the day you started. You are not at fault. You are a victim, and you must fight for your survival. You are a victim of verbal and emotional abuse. The sooner you depart the better. No amount of money is worth the abuse you will endure.

As an unselfish leader, you should realize that you are hiring people who might be coming to you from such a tragic situation. They are afraid, timid, and untrusting for good reason. A quality leader recognizes that not all new hires come in the door as whole people. They have been damaged. You are an essential part of the healing process. Speaking from experience, not many leaders are aware of this. But if you have been through it, then you are. How can an unselfish leader tell? If your new hire is quiet, and reserved to the point of not sharing their thoughts. If they ask you for approval for things they should be normally doing, this is a good indication they have been under a micromanager. If they arrive at work an hour before they start and wait for permission to leave at the end of the day, then they have been under the dominance of a micromanager.

How do you help them to heal? I must say that this won't always be a successful endeavor, and I have found out that some can be so damaged by a micromanager that they never fully recover. I hired a person who had worked for the post office and was micromanaged for years. She had a difficult time being on her own and working in a relaxed environment. She told me one day that employees were not working as hard as they should. I told her that that was not her decision to make. I also told her that I appreciated how she worked, and that she was a great example to others. She was impatient with staff and customers. She blew up one day about a customer, and I sat her down and tried to get to the bottom of her behavior. I asked her what concerned her, and she told me that she'd worked at the post office for 20 years and it was high pressure, so adjusting was hard. I reassured her that this was not the post office and she could simply relax and do her job. I asked how could I help? I also apologized for what she had been through.

I thought we were good, but her next response took me by surprise. She stated that I was not a good supervisor because people were not working fast and were talking too much while they worked. I told her that talking while you work does not violate a policy. I asked her to take a few days with pay to reevaluate why she wants to work here. The following week I got a call telling me she was quitting. It was too relaxed an atmosphere for her. I felt so sorry for her. She was a victim of a micromanager whose lasting impact was so great that she could not overcome it. When she left, she gave me a sweet poem about love and thanked me for all I did for her. As an unselfish leader, I think about her often and wonder what I could have done to help her heal.

One of the most difficult things to confront is the idea that you can't help or lead everyone. An unselfish leader wants the best for everyone. There is no exception to this rule. We want those we lead to be healthy and happy. We want them to smile and to feel appreciated. We want them to love what they do and value every aspect of it. Maybe this seems to be a pipe dream, but I have had the fortune of being in a space like this. In the work environment and also in life, there is no greater feeling than knowing that people trust and believe in you. These unselfish leaders give you latitude to be creative and they value your input. Being a valued member of the team is a remarkable feeling.

I believe being a micromanager is symptomatic of one's view of life. Its origin lies deep within the crevasses of a person's character. As the title of this chapter states, it's all about control. They view a world (their world) that must be controlled. To allow for you to have some control, or to do a thing without their permission produces heights of anxiety and fear for them. Allowing you to give them direction or to make the final decision are beyond their comfort zone. The only world that matters to them is one in which they control. Whether it's in their personal life or at their job, and sometimes at their places of worship, they must be in charge. In their minds, there is only one way to think, do, or try anything, and it's their way. I must repeat, I strongly advise that if you find yourself under such leadership, you find another place of employment; or, if this is a social or romantic relationship, find a way to end it as soon as possible. You will never win them over, and eventually they will suck all the life out of you.

Scenario: *Micromanager*

Your supervisor gives you a task that really requires only your efforts to complete. Yet she insists that you work with others in the office to complete the task. She goes as far as to tell you how to work with others and what working with them should look like. She wants to attend every meeting during the process and wants you to give her a written report on every meeting as soon as it ends. You try to suggest some ideas, but those are quickly discounted.

What steps, if any, can you take to get her to see that she is micromanaging you?

_____

_____

_____

_____

_____

_____

_____

_____

_____

Being under the control of a micromanager is one of the hardest places to land in the workplace. What is the cost that you are willing to pay to endure this abuse? Whatever it is, I suggest that the price is too high! As a person who deserves to be valued, appreciated, and respected, I urge you to move on to a better situation. In the end, you are moving on to a better life!

"Practice self-awareness, self-evaluation, and self-improvement. If we are aware that our manners - language, behavior, and actions - are measured against our values and principles, we are able to more easily embody the philosophy, leadership is a matter of how to be, not how to do."-
Frances Hesselbein

Chapter 9
Culture

Oftentimes we stay at or leave a job depending on the condition of its culture. Organizational Culture is defined as "the customs, rituals, and values shared by the members of an organization that have to be accepted by new members."[36] Notice quickly that these customs, rituals, and values are shared by all involved. How can you share in a culture that devalues you or marginalizes your participation in it? "In a company or corporation, its culture is demonstrated by its management style, including the degree of autocracy or participation practiced, and the expectations of employees."[37]

Let's examine a culture that is dictated by autocracy.

Under an autocratic leadership, the person in change has unlimited control over those who work for them. There is no accountability for the leader's actions or decisions. We find this very commonly among private companies and nonprofits. Small but growing mom-and-pop companies that bring on new employees resist letting those outside of the established circle in. Very often, these are family-owned businesses which one or two people created, and they maintain complete control of the operations. Imagine being hired on to work in this autocratic environment. It is probably widely known among the family members employed there that either dad or mom makes all the decisions. I've been here too. In this environment, no one disagrees or initiates anything out of fear of being reprimanded.

[36] Dictionary.com, s.v., "citation," accessed September 13, 2018, https://www.dictionary.com/browse/culture?s=t.
[37] Michael Murphy et al., "Stress and Organizational Culture," *The British Journal of Social Work* 26, no. 5 (October 1996): 648.

This was my first real job, and I was so excited to get it. I quickly observed that you were only supposed to do what you were told, and that questioning anything was definitely costly to your psychological health. As a matter of fact, the very notion that you could be fired at any given moment lingered in the air. I remember calling in sick one day and the boss flat out told me, "If you don't come in today, then don't come back." An autocratic leader's only concern is getting things done his way. As we discussed in a previous chapter, control can be a dangerous thing. Put better, seeking total dominance over people is pathological and unacceptable.

I ran into this again later in my career. As a high-level director, I encountered this situation again in a nonprofit organization. Although it was more subtle than the previous described situation, the results were the same. I had no autonomy. I am not totally convinced that these autocratic leaders are aware of this destructive behavior. I think they have been controlling and dictating so long that it has become a management style for them (or the lack thereof). If you have ever been in a situation like this, you know the devastation it can cause for all involved.

Participating in helping to create and sustain an organization's culture is where you want to be. From the start, you have an established agreement on what the organization's culture is and what it is not. Furthermore, you can agree upon the list of values accepted and rejected. However, most of us don't have the luxury of creating the culture. More than likely, we find ourselves walking into a "created culture."

I want to give you 7 things to look for when you walk into a created culture:

1. Is it a high pressure, results-only operation?
2. How does the supervisor communicate to the staff?
3. Does she welcome input and disagreements?
4. Do people feel comfortable speaking up?
5. Do employees gossip?
6. Are people warning you about others in the organization?
7. Is there high employee turnover?

These 7 sample questions will give you a pretty good picture of the culture you have just joined or are contemplating joining.

Although management should help reinforce the culture, they should not be the sole creator of it. Organizational culture should be "the sum total of the values, beliefs and ideologies of the people who make up the organization. As such, it cannot be changed by management edict but has to be crafted, carefully shaped and molded through negotiation..."[38] When I speak on culture, you will undoubtedly hear me say that we make up the culture. Think of this as you would the larger society's culture. It is the people who create, shape, and mold it. For instance, jazz culture is made up of a plethora of musicians, producers, record companies, and ultimately the fans. No one party can create this. So why do we leave it up to one or two people to determine our values and customs in the workplace? It seems quite silly when you look at it like that.

Creating and maintaining a culture is a complex endeavor. Beyond being complexed, it has many layers, and these layers must be blended together

---

[38] Michael Murphy et. al, 647.

"What we describe as the culture, in fact, is an amalgam of various cultures or sub-cultures which operate within the organization. These sub-cultures are often a source of conflict and tension within the organization.[39] If you work in a diverse environment, which I hope you do, then you are experiencing multiple-cultural exchanges every day. These exchanges are the layers I mentioned above. A workplace should not be monolithic. The world we live in is not monolithic. We don't all think alike and see the world through the same lens.

I spent 13 years in the Navy, and that was about as close to a monolithic culture as I have experienced. We dressed alike, followed the same rules, adhered to the same values and customs, but understand, this was an autocratic organization. It works because of the need to perform and get results which, if not achieved, could end up in a loss of life. The military is a fine-tuned organization that relies upon a strict adherence to rules and regulations. Again, to violate them could cause the death of someone. So, it is necessary for the military to have a culture that reflects these practices. When we are sailing through the vast ocean, there isn't time to debate when something goes wrong. We are trained to react to save lives and preserve vital equipment. Those outside of the military are not under this type of day-to-day pressure. And I think most of us with the exception of law enforcement, emergency care services, and the like don't work in life and death situations; therefore, the interplay of our experiences should shape and mold our workplaces.

---

[39] Michael Murphy et. al, 648.

As mentioned above, these sub-cultures can be a source of tension. When you bring people together who are from various regions of the country or the world, and/or with different cultural or ethnic backgrounds, along with differences in age and gender, you are bound to have some conflict. The U.S. Military is all about conformity for good reason, but in civilian life, it's the blending of all these sub-cultures that makes life interesting and challenging. I think too many leaders simply want employees to conform to an established set of values and customs. While in some cases this might work out well, more than likely you will have to deal with rising conflict. An unselfish leader understands this potential and when it occurs, addresses it head on. Do you really believe that a man who grew up on the south side of Chicago views the world the same way as a woman who grew up in Atherton, California, the richest suburb in America? These two individuals will undoubtedly approach decision-making differently, and they might even have different value systems, regardless of who may be right or wrong.

Yet they both play a role in shaping and molding the organization's culture. I worked with an older man who could not tolerate what he perceived as the lack of commitment of a younger staff member. I asked him one day, "Do you remember what you were like at his age?" He replied, "It doesn't matter; he needs to learn." I marveled at his statement. If he really cared about this young man, why didn't he mentor him instead of being so critical? One day I asked him to do just that – be a mentor to this young man – but he clearly had no interest in that role. I think the older gentleman was simply taken back by his coworker's playful attitude. On the other hand, I rather enjoyed the unassuming nature this young man had, and the calmness he brought to the workplace. This was clearly a generational difference.

The old man got up, came to work, worked hard, and stayed late. He saw this as commitment. The young man came to work, worked his pace, and went home as soon as he could. The old man's identity was wrapped up in his work. The young man's identity was wrapped up in his life outside of work. The supervisor over this department did a terrible job of blending these value systems together. The young man eventually quit and moved on. He got tired of being judged by the old man. This happens too often in our workplaces. If we truly make up the culture, then tension and conflict are part of the creative process, and we should not avoid it.

In order to create a healthy organizational culture, it must be a culture of commitment and not compliance. Recall the military discussion. The military is a culture of compliance and when someone doesn't comply, it can be costly for the people with whom they serve. This knowledge, in turn, keeps others in compliance. My first managing job outside of the Navy was in the manufacturing industry. One day, we had a chemical spill that I asked a few of my staff members to clean up. About 10 minutes into the job, the break bell sounded and I made my way to the area of the spill. To my surprise, no one was there. I went to my boss complaining that they'd left without finishing the job. He responded, "Michael, this is not the military. People have rights and by law, they can take their scheduled break." I felt very foolish, but it was a learning experience for me. This organization had a culture of commitment and not compliance. By the way, people in the military do have rights, and we would have finished the job before taking a break – just a side note.

By backing the workers, my boss taught me a very valuable lesson. This was an agreed-upon value and one that I came to honor and respect. In a culture of compliance, the employees would have received punitive consequences for their actions. In an autocratic environment, they might have been fired. Of course, the old man in the previous scenario would have called them lazy and uncommitted. Yet no lives were at stake, and once off their break, they finished the job in no time. I would eventually learn that these individuals were some of the most committed people in my department. A culture of commitment is based upon shared values, respect, and consideration for all who help to maintain the culture.

By contrast, you may find yourself walking into a negative culture. A negative culture is defined as "a culture which is defensive, counterproductive, and dysfunctional for the organization as a whole."[40] It's defensive because the leadership may be autocratic or the leadership maybe centralized. A centralized leadership group makes all the decisions at the top. Under these administrations, if you make a decision or attempt to do something without their approval, you are punished. Power is concentrated at the top. Under leadership like this, it is extremely problematic for middle managers. The pressure of trying to empower those who work for you, while handling the pressure of a centralized power structure above you, can be overwhelming even for the wisest leader.

---

[40] Michael Murphy et. al, 650.

A negative culture is defensive because new ideas are not welcome, and every decision is made by a centralized leadership, which can be as small as one or two people. Staff members are not rewarded, but punished for their creativity and innovation. As the saying goes, "No good deed goes unpunished." They are defensive because any disagreement with those in charge is seen as disloyal or a challenge to their authority. A negative culture is counterproductive because of its resistance to change. Change is the only constant in our lives. As human beings, we are changing every day. Technology, politics, governments, music and the likes are constantly changing. How can an organization be successful if it does not change? We cannot be successful. We lose our creative desires when we are immovable. We lose perspective when we think we have all the answers. Change brings growth and productivity. A new product, a new technology to learn, a new idea, or learning a different way to make what you currently do better all require us to change.

Organizations become counterproductive when they refuse to change. They refuse to change out of fear of the unknown. Unselfish leadership is about leading people into the unknown. Isn't this the definition of vision? I have seen it time and time again – organizations paralyzed by fear. They stay far from the cutting edge and become irrelevant in an ever-changing world. Employees cannot thrive in counterproductive environments. Sooner or later, complicity sets in and people simply go through the routine of their day. The great mission that these organizations have are relegated to the paper they were printed on. A culture of counterproductivity leads to high turnover and unmotivated personnel.

Remember that dysfunctionality and counterproductivity leads to what researchers call "learned helplessness." This is "a psychological state which results when a person perceives that he can no longer control his own destiny."[41] When a culture creates an atmosphere of learned helplessness, employees no longer feel like they make contributions to the mission. They lose their passion for the work, lack physical and creative energy for the work, and ultimately give up. They become the working dead, but you don't recognize it. You note it as compliance. In this scenario, no one complains, no one speaks up. No one offers a different opinion or seeks to offer new ideas. People simply go with the flow. This environment kills the soul and rewards the company with the highest form of inefficiency as possible.

Please recall that "culture relates to shared values, meanings and symbols. We can see a situation in which a negative culture that has evolved could be a very destructive one for the staff concerned, as well as the organization and its service users, as low morale saps motivation, commitment, creativity and job satisfaction."[42] For the leader walking into such an environment, it is difficult to combat. Do you leave or do you try to change the trajectory of the culture? An unselfish leader cares about people and does not give up easily. In this situation, you must try to propel the organization in the right direction. I am not so naïve to think that you will always be successful, but one who does not try will never succeed.

---

[41] Michael Murphy et. al, 651.
[42] Michael Murphy et. al, 652.

As unselfish leaders, we must help build healthy cultures that are inclusive and ones that empower everyone in the group. If you are in a leadership role, hopefully you have helped to create and maintain a vibrant culture. If not, I suggest you examine the condition of the existing culture at your workplace and employ new ideas to change it. Look again at the 7 things you should observe as you walk into a created culture and evaluate your present situation. Remember, culture is created and sustained by everyone in the organization, if it is not autocratic. Be the leader that heals the broken and encourages the frail among you. You can be that leader. You can be the one that others aspire to become. Why would we spend the majority of our lives at work and choose to spend it in an unhealthy culture? It doesn't make sense when you look at it through this lens.

Don't let others tell you that this is the way things should be. Don't settle for the old school approach of "no pain, no gain." We can gain so much without the psychological pain and stress that so many people are experiencing. There are situations in which the culture will not change. For instance, in a work culture with a leader or employees who are sociopathic, there will be no charge. No matter what you try, such people don't have the capacity to empathize or compromise. As an unselfish leader, you might have to purge such individuals to create a healthy atmosphere. I know this sounds harsh, but do not be deceived – these moments will arise.

I want to talk about the consequences of creating a toxic culture, and those individuals who do not buy into a healthy culture. We are all familiar with the phrase "going postal." It pains me to address this topic; however, to ignore it would be unwise. We have seen disgruntled employees come into the workplace and take innocent life. Oftentimes the individual is painted as a mad person and dismissed as someone unhinged. But I argue that the situation is more complicated than that. Because most of these atrocities are carried out with a gun, a gun debate is the predominant response. Yes, a gun debate is necessary, but we must dig deeper.

What drives a person to the point at which he is willing to take the lives of his coworkers? This is the important question to ask. Now, because of employee record confidential regulations, we don't get the inside scoop. So, what is the cause? I don't profess to be an expert, but I believe it has a lot to do with the culture of the work environment. This suggestion might make some uneasy. No one should ever use violence to solve a problem, yet we have found that several do. A bad work culture inflicts pain and stress on workers. I have been there, although I would never have resorted to those measures like some fragile people have.

It's important that we recognize the impact that unhealthy cultures have on the fragile among us. I want you to consider that we don't know what's going on in the private lives of employees. For instance, there may be an impending divorce, a death in the family, a rebellious child, or a history of mental illness, to name a few. What impact does a negative work culture contribute? Although we try hard to separate the personal from the professional, oftentimes they get blended. The agitated employee is responding partly because of the pressures outside of the job. Her anger is not directed towards you. The pains of life have overflowed into the work environment. An unselfish leader is quite aware of this potential.

Yet there are situations in which the workplace is the cause of this distress. It is the autocratic boss or the micromanager who has created a toxic environment. The actions of these individuals place everyone in danger. While it is possible to ignore a toxic manager's behavior, you may be placing yourself in danger by doing so. It is important to speak up and hold everyone to the standard articulated by the organization. It may save lives. Let me be clear. I am not in any way condoning these acts, yet there are reasons why people explode in the workplace, and not every breakdown can be attributed to their private lives or mental health. Speak up when you see a coworker wronged or abused. If your coworker is being abused, so are you. We are a team. If a basketball team loses, the whole team loses. No one walks away with the loss alone. It is a team effort, so please don't leave a fragile teammate out there by himself.

In my final analysis of it all, an unselfish leader must get to know those of whom they are in charge. There is no exception to this rule. You should know their aspirations, challenges at work, and things they are willing to share regarding their personal lives. We are the bridge between harmony and insanity. I know that's a challenging statement, but don't discount the enormity of it. In the modern era, a leader can hold the power of life and death in her hands. The power to breathe life into a vulnerable soul, or the power to crush the self-esteem of those she is entrusted to govern. I suggest that you choose life.

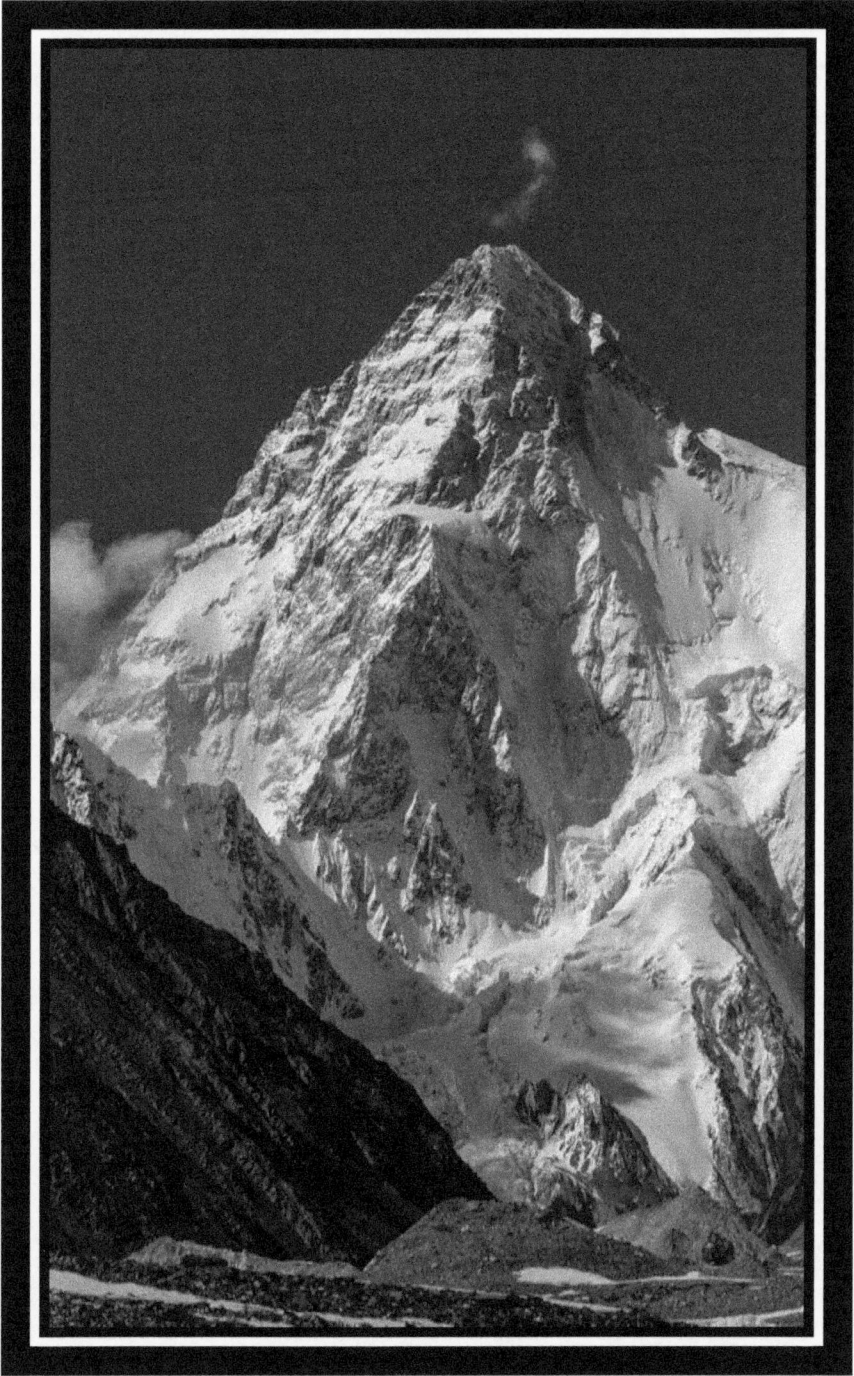

Chapter 10
Organizational Goals

What are organizational goals? They are defined as "strategic objectives that a company's management establishes to outline expected outcomes and guide employees' efforts."[43] Organizational goals are codified by the company's leadership. However, they are designed to guide the employee's work and productivity. Without an employee's clear understanding of the role he plays towards the achievement of these goals, the goals will never be reached. "Clear organizational goals can drive employee efforts throughout the organization… Communicating organizational goals to employees is essential for achieving those desired outcomes."[44] Yet, printing them in a brochure or employee handbook does not constitute engagement.

Workers need to be engaged in the philosophy that created the goals in the first place. As leaders, it is important to communicate how beneficial the workers' efforts are in assisting the company to achieve them. The goals need to be "specific, measurable, achievable and timely. By setting clear, realistic goals, organizations have a clearer path to achieve success and realize its vision. Goal setting, and attaining them, can also help an organization achieve increased efficiency, productivity and profitability."[45] This is where many companies fail. They fail because the goals are not

[43] TechTarget, "Operational Goals." https://searchcio.techtarget.com/definition/organizational-goals.

[44] Office of Performance Management. "Organizational Goals Can Be Powerful Energizers." https://www.opm.gov/policy-data-oversight/performance-management/performance-management-cycle/planning/organizational-goals-can-be-powerful-energizers/.

[45] TechTarget.

realistic or clear. In some cases, they fail because the goals are fluid; this creates instability.

I have participated in my share of strategic planning sessions. Groups spend all day strategizing and categorizing their goals, only to never to return to them until the annual planning session. Other teams spend all day setting goals and developing flowcharts, and a month later, arrange a planning session with completely different objectives in mind. "Often, groups and organizations participate in team building and strategic off-sites only to have the momentum lost because there is no plan for ongoing follow-up."[46] I worked for one company where this was the practice and not the exception. Many on the staff were so confused because we did not know what goals we were currently working on. In situations like these, frustration sets in. I felt like a ship adrift, being tossed to and fro by the waves with no destination in sight.

Once a company has established their organizational goals, communicated them clearly, and set in place measures to achieve them, they must engage their workers. In his article "Just Care More," Brian McNamara introduces an approach to engaging staff members, called the CARE approach. The CARE approach consists of the following:

"Create, communicate, and implement a vision.
    Ask questions and listen.
    Respect and value others.
    Encourage and support growth and development."[47]

---

[46] Brian McNamara, "Just Care More," *Talent Development*. November 2018: 54.
[47] Brian McNamara, "Just Care More." 54.

We have spent some time talking about creating a vision, communicating it, and the importance of implementing it. Yet, these efforts are mostly one-sided; therefore, I consider this to be the beginning stages of engagement. As Mr. McNamara has pointed out, in order to engage people, you must ask questions and listen to their responses. I don't mean having a forum or any type of group meeting. I am talking about one-on-one engagement. A selfish leader sees this as a waste of time. An unselfish leader sees this as the only way to get to know those who work for you. In other words, this is the only engagement that matters – asking and listening. In a few minutes, you will discover that following through completes the circle of engagement.

I often spend time simply asking staff about their life, their family, their goals, and their dreams. I see value in knowing who they are and understanding what makes them tick. However, you will never get true engagement if they don't trust you. Too many managers ask questions in order to find a weakness or gain some sort of leverage over an employee. If your staff do not trust you, you will only get the answer they anticipate you are after. Trust and engagement go hand in hand. You ask because you care. You ask because you want them to know that they have value and their thoughts matter. If you don't know them, how can you guide them through the goals of the organization?

The majority of us can recognize when someone is being genuine. And we can definitely point out a fake. "Trust is delicate to manage within any workplace. It can take a long time to establish but only moments to destroy."[48] Think about that one. It can take only a moment to destroy. This is the leading reason companies do not achieve their organizational goals: mistrust. If you never follow through on your employees' concerns, this sends a message that, at best, you are not listening, and at worst, you don't care. Either one of those scenarios destroys trust. Do you want to try to achieve your day-to-day goals with someone you can't trust?

Ask questions that show a deep interest in your employee. Be more than a superficial person. I will admit that not all your workers will be comfortable sharing their life with you. I consider myself a private person; you must respect the privacy of others. Oftentimes this reluctance comes from being hurt in the past. It comes from the destructive behavior of a selfish leader in their past. It's not fair, but we must contend with the pain caused by others and the havoc it continues to wreak on their lives. So, move slow with these fragile hearts and let trust build up over time. They will come around... if – and only if – you can be found trustworthy.

Listening requires attentive silence. Few in our world have the ability to remain silent. We live in a world in which the one who's the loudest, and so often, the rudest, gets the most attention. I'm asking you to be an engaged and gentle listener. Try to stay still and thoughtful in these moments. Our minds wander because we are inundated with information, and the demands of daily life can be overwhelming. Yet we must learn to become attentive listeners. Meaning, you are actively listening to the person in front of you.

---

[48] Brian McNamara, "Just Care More." 55.

If you are departmentalizing this moment, then they will have your undivided attention. Can you do this?

How do you actively listen?

_____

_____

_____

_____

_____

_____

A person actively listens by providing feedback and validating the speaker. You don't devalue or discount what a person is saying, even if you don't agree with the statement. I remember, after a long day of reflecting on last year's accomplishments and planning next year's goals, I was asked, "How did you think today's sessions went?" When I returned with my honest reply, the one who asked immediately told me he disagreed with me. I was not asking this of him; it was he who asked for my opinion. We often shut people down when they don't give the answer we are looking for. Even though we have established organizational goals, we should from time to time inquire of our staff to help us reevaluate these goals. I was asked one day, "Why should lower-level people be included in the process of goal setting?" I replied, "Because they are the ones doing the work." Selfish leaders don't listen because they don't want feedback and they don't want to be challenged. In the military this strategy works well, but in the civilian world, it is unrealistic and, most importantly, unproductive. Companies that don't listen or ask the right questions of their employees have high turnover and are completely unstable. If you never include them, they will never claim ownership of the company's goals. And if you don't listen, they will stop talking. A non-communicative workforce is a dead workforce. Trust me, they will simply go through the motions until something better comes along. They will sit in the planning session, smile, and even respond (with what they think you want to hear) when called upon.

As an unselfish leader, we recognize that engagement on our part guarantees involvement on their part. I was asked during an interview for a director's position, what was my vision for the organization? I always find this to be an awkward question. The organization already had a vision, so are they expecting me to come in and change what has been agreed upon? I replied, "I can't answer that question. You have a vision, which I truly like, and my approach is to include staff in the crafting of a vision. They must be included, so if I am hired, after consulting with staff, I can better answer that question." I did not get the job. And I count it a blessing. I only want to work for an organization that understands the value of including everyone when formulating a new vision or organizational goals.

Remember, I said that asking and listening are important. But if you don't follow through on the information received, you'll be viewed as uncaring. An unselfish leader knows follow-through completes the *circle of listening*. Yes, I want you to think of it as a circle. You start by asking questions, you listen and provide feedback, and then you follow through. When you follow through, it does not mean that you do exactly what is requested. Input or requests cannot be honored if they do not align with organizational goals.

Recall, organizational goals are a guide for the day-to-day operations of the organization and its employees. Think of organizational goals as your GPS. It is your coordinates and provides a step by step logical direction for getting where you are trying to go.

So, if an employee's request or input would steer you off course, you explain why it would not be the best course of action. Look at the follow-through as a teachable moment for your staff. They will respect you for that. But if you simply say, "No, we can't do that," then you appear uncaring. Incidentally, a "no" isn't always verbal or stated directly. A "no" expressed by a leader often appears in the form of talking over, ignoring, or not acknowledging the input staff members have offered. In either case, they leave wondering why did you ask them in the first place. An unselfish leader always stands prepared to answer the "Why not?" question. In moments like these, you can build trust by showing others you care enough to provide feedback rather than simply saying no, or because "I don't want to do that." The latter is a deflating statement and you should never use it. When I give no as an answer, I always provide an alternative to the suggestion. This makes it clear that I've listened, thought about it, and cared enough to provide feedback we both could live with.

I was at a seminar when the facilitator asked us to write down our definition of respect. I thought this was a very simple thing to do, but in that room were multiple ideas regarding the word. I quickly noticed that our life experiences and backgrounds dictated how we each defined the concept of respect.

How would you define Respect?

_____

_____

_____

_____

_____

_____

For me, respect has a lot to do with how I want to be treated and how I treat others. It means that I am listened to and my views are validated and considered. It means I am spoken to in a professional manner, and I able to sense that I matter to you and the organization. It also means that I expect to be treated fairly and given the same rights and privileges as anyone else in the workplace. I was told one time that a staff member was "so disrespectful." I asked the boss why he felt that way. He replied, "Because she has something to say every time I say we have to do this or that." What *he* was truly saying is, "Anyone who questions me or disagrees with me is being disrespectful." A lot of leaders in our world today believe just like this supervisor.

As unselfish leaders, we understand that respecting people is an important aspect of leadership. Although you may disagree, you never let it become so personal that you attack a person's character. I call these types of attacks *value judgements*. A value judgement is when criticism is attached to a person's character. When the completion of a task is what signifies whether a person is a good person or a bad person. For example, statements like, "If

he were raised better, he would have supported you better at the meeting."
I will suggest that supporting a person or not has nothing to do with your
upbringing. Or something like, "Her parents must have never taught her
accountability." These are value judgements that question the character of
a person. Furthermore, they are based on skewed ideas, and we have no
way of knowing whether or not they are true. It's just meanspirited and
disrespectful. If you talk like this, the rest of your team will follow your
lead. This will chip away at a healthy culture.

Have you ever worked for someone you thought did not respect you? Well,
I have… It's a terrible feeling, and it's hard not to take it personally. I think
a disrespectful person does not respect anyone, so taking it personally
causes more damage to us than to them. Yet I know it's hard not to be
impacted by such horrid behavior. What do you do in a situation like this,
or what if you observe that someone else is being disrespected? I was having
lunch with a colleague and she started saying some very ugly things about
her boss. Now, I was introduced to this colleague by her boss, a woman
with whom I also happened to be good friends. I reminded this colleague of
my friendship, and also expressed that it was disrespectful for her to speak
this way about her boss. I reminded her that she was not in charge;
therefore, if she had these concerns, she should have a conversation directly
with *her*. I sensed that she did not enjoy my feedback. It's important that
we always be respectful and that we stand up for those who are being
disrespected.

A good leader believes fundamentally that regardless of one's race, creed,
gender, age, appearance, or sexual orientation, all people deserve to be

treated with respect. You refuse to make value judgements. You do not attack a person's character and make him feel ashamed for who he is. None of us would appreciate this type of attack, so let's not do things to others that we don't want done to us. I don't know why so many people find this hard to accomplish in their leadership role. We should be the first to create a respectful environment and the first to challenge all who seek to dismantle it.

What are the attributes of a respectful person? Kindness, empathy, sincerity, and patience. Their tone is soothing and not harsh. They are quick to understand and even quicker in offering forgiveness. A lot of supervisors think that being harsh and direct are good signs of effective leadership. I have heard more than once, "She is tough on her staff, but she gets the job done." This is another way of saying that someone is rude and disrespectful, but they are able to get the company's work done. Is simply getting the work done your litmus test for reaching organizational goals? If so, you are not an unselfish leader. It's not about getting it done, it's about *how* you get the job done. No one wants to spend eight hours of his day under the leadership of a disrespectful person. As soon as something remotely better comes along, he will jump ship. When people are respected, they feel valued. And when people feel valued, they remain productive in the workplace.

The last aspect of the CARE approach is: Encouragement, Support Growth and Development. "People want to contribute and make a difference, know that what they do matters, and be involved in something greater than themselves."[49] An unselfish leader wants his crew members to reach their full potential and sees a role in ensuring this. Are you an encourager? Do you know what that entails? At the core, it's about finding ways to empower people. Do you believe in your employees? You must, in order to help them. It's not where they start, but where they end up. Help them reach their personal goals while they are working towards achieving the organization's goals. This is not a zero-sum game. Find out what their personal goals are in and out of the organization. Use your influence and contacts to support their growth. A person who lives a happy and content life outside of work will mimic this in the workplace.

Remember, people want to be part of something greater than themselves. My mother was a great leader. She would always encourage me, and she would support whatever wild dream I conjured up. Some I succeeded at and others I didn't, but she never discouraged me. We must have the same approach as leaders. Our workers' success is our success. We rejoice in helping them reach for the stars. We encourage and support because it is the righteous thing to do. I am speaking about an unselfish act. We take no glory away from them. As a matter of fact, we celebrate them. If an employee wants to be promoted, build a path for upward mobility with him. If someone has a new initiative that falls within the organizational goals, employ it. If it fails, so what. If you never take a risk, you will never be

---

[49] Brian McNamara, "Just Care More." 54.

successful. Some of the greatest successes in life have come by way of failure.

An unselfish leader does not want people to stay where they are. She desires for them to learn, grow, and excel. She believes in them and reminds them of their value to the organization and its goals. I stated earlier that a good leader is an encourager, but she is also a visionary. She does not just have a vision for herself, but for those she leads. She is able to birth a vision in them and help them strategize ways to bring this vision to life. If they fail, you fail together and you rise again together. As you seek to achieve organizational goals, please remember that those working with you are looking towards you to encourage, support, and help them in their personal development.

Chapter 11
Can You Trust HR?

We come to a very important question for every employee to answer. Can you trust those in your Human Resource Department (HR)? If you are an HR Director or work in the HR Department, I will introduce this caveat: this indictment is not intended for those who support, advocate, and apply justice for all; however, it is intended for those who do not. While I have not conducted a scientific survey, most of the people I encounter whom I ask whether or not they trust their HR, answer most certainly no. Why is that? I think most people working in this field are just like most of us. They are afraid of losing their jobs. Upper management bullies them and strips them of their power. But most importantly, I think we have the wrong perception of who they are and whom they represent.

As a young person entering the workforce, I was told that HR was there for the employees. You would think this is the case because they are the first people you meet. They assist you in filling out the hiring paperwork and, in some companies, they are the ones who interview you. They help you sign up for the proper benefits, schedule your initial trainings, and they ensure you get paid. They are the friendly face you encounter when you arrive for your first day of work. Why wouldn't you think they are there for you? They will tell you that if you need anything please don't hesitate to contact them, and now off you go! This experience gives employees a false sense of the HR-employee relationship. To be totally honest with you, there is no HR-employee "relationship." Or, better put, the relationship is contractual.

I think the human condition makes it easy for us to forget that we are there to fulfill a written, agreed-upon contract. Which, in essence, states that if you do this work, we will pay you this amount of money. It's just that simple. However, we are people and most of us are relational. Why do we need an HR Department?

It is documented that "human resources departments started in the early 1900s when companies were trying to figure out how to reduce turnover and maximize performance through new compensation systems. The HR staff would conduct exit interviews and collect grievances about issues that caused companies to lose employees or led to unionization efforts."[50] HR was created because of people quitting their jobs, high turnover, and job dissatisfaction.

On one level, I find it comforting to know that this is not a new problem that we are facing, but on another level, I find it horrifying that we have not solved the problem of workers feeling devalued, overlooked, marginalized, and on and on. Notice that HR was not formed to keep employees satisfied, but to learn why they were not. However, the role of HR began to change in the 1930s. "By the 1930s human resources started to become and be seen as advocates for employees and the reason for that, frankly, was because companies were trying to keep unions out."[51] This is an important shift to note. The need to be seen as an advocate for workers arose to ward off the rise in union representation. So, HR's initial purpose was to find out why workers were leaving, and then in the 1930s, it was deployed to prevent

---

[50] Jana Kasperkevic. "HR is not there to be your friend. It's there to protect the company." https://www.marketplace.org/2017/10/30/human-resources-protect-employee-employer/.
[51] Jana Kasperkevic. "HR is not there to be your friend. It's there to protect the company."

workers from seeking outside representation. Both of these purposes have the company's interest as priority. Now, I'm not advocating that the company's interest should not be important. I'm simply pointing out the fact that HR wasn't created to be your friend.

I think we would agree that there has been an all-out war against unions in our country. "In the 1980s, union membership began to drop off and companies no longer wanted to hear about what people wanted. They had other things to worry about – like making sure that they were complying with all of the new worker protection laws that were being passed. By that period, HR's mandate kind of shifted to protecting the company..."[52] I think we find ourselves in the same position today. Most of HR is designed to protect the company, but what are they protecting the company from?

They protect the company by ensuring that all policies and procedures are codified. They protect the company by making sure all employees complete their mandatory training on time. I worked for a company in which the only time we would hear from the supervisor or HR was when people were not completing their monthly training. The threats would fly, and it didn't matter what the issue was – training had to be completed. You'd have to have been on your deathbed to be excused, and then they might have brought that ole VHS sexual harassment tape to your hospital room for you to watch to get it done. At this particular company, HR's role was that of a protector. There were multiple incidences of abuse of power, creating a

---

[52] Jana Kasperkevic, "HR is not there to be your friend. It's there to protect the company."

hostile work environment, and downright unfair practices, but the HR department, like many today, looked the other way from such abuses. HR is there to protect the company and not you. I think some HR personnel believe in the philosophy that you are replaceable, but the company will always be there.

Listen, why should HR care? Why should they support you or listen to you? You don't pay their salaries. They don't report to you. They have seen people come and go, so what makes you so special? Why should they be your friend?

As an unselfish leader, it is important to understand the dynamic at play here. Now, leadership does not require that you befriend a coworker – and, let's face it, no matter how hard we try, we will not make friends with everyone we meet. However, the role of HR and leadership is more than simply protecting the company. On the shelves and in their databases are policies and procedures that protect the company and its employees. The problem occurs when the company becomes more vital than those who comprise it. How would Microsoft stock trade if all of its employees walked out today or they all filed grievances against their supervisors, and the world heard about it on CNN?

I find it very unpleasant and counterproductive when the concerns of employees are ignored. Too often HR is not independent from upper management. It is more of an extension of it. HR Managers and Directors are terrified to bring an accusation against upper management. Many HR personnel are trying to fit in and secure their own position within the company. You, my friend, are an unpleasant distraction who needs to be marginalized, silenced, or, worst-case scenario, fired. I worked for a small nonprofit in which the Chief Financial Officer (CFO) was also the entire HR Department. She was extremely protective of the boss. As a matter of fact, she and the boss were instrumental in creating the employee handbook and all the policies and procedures for the organization.

Everyone knew that if you talked to her, you were talking directly to the boss. When I heard that the CFO was over HR, I thought it was a joke, but no – she was. Needless to say, there were no employee concerns ever reported. Too many organizations practice this method of Human Resources. When the administration and HR become inseparable, you have a major problem. Where can you turn when an injustice happens in the organization and HR is in the hip pocket of upper admin? These are important questions, and I hope you don't find yourselves in this situation. If you do, then I can only hope that you have an exit plan.

As an unselfish leader, you must understand the dynamics I've just described. What role do you play when you find yourself or an employee you supervise in this dire state? An unselfish leader always seeks justice regardless of the cost to one's person or livelihood. In other words, you place the employee above the cost to yourself. Further, you recognize that your response and your actions will make it either easier for those who come behind you or more difficult. I recall working for a company in which I had to file a grievance against a supervisor, and the other directors came to me and thanked me for standing up. I asked them why? They replied that this had been going on for years and they were too afraid to stand up. Well, that certainly put a spin on what they'd meant as a compliment. I let them know that I was going through this *because* they were too afraid to do anything about it when it happened to them. If they had of taken a stand years ago, I might not have had to deal with the unpleasantness – putting it mildly – of that season. You can make a difference if you do the right thing.

From time to time, a difficult situation will occur under your watch. If this were not the case, you would not find policies for dealing with them. It is important that an unselfish leader completely understand the rights of the employees he supervises. It also critical that a polished leader figures out how to navigate a relationship between HR and the administration. Recall the chapter of Buffering... Reread it if necessary. Some of the strategies in that chapter can also be helpful here. Oftentimes, you are the complete support structure for the wronged employee. An employee who has leveled a charge against someone in the organization can feel all alone. I have personally seen coworkers scatter from that person out of fear of being caught in the impending wake.

So how do you respond when you or one of your employees is that person grieved by a superior? First, I always encourage employees to document communication whether it occurred in person, via phone conversation, or in email. I have made that suggestion even to those I supervise. Secondly, use that documentation to have a conversation with the person you are having concerns about. When you approach them, come to the meeting with your documentation, reasons for your concerns, and solution to alleviate them. Hopefully, you will have a successful outcome. If not, I really encourage you to keep HR involved. However, remember they are there to protect the company, so be careful and deliberate that your documentation describes violations against company policy. Your response cannot be personal. It must line up with the do's and don'ts of the organization. This is the only way you will get traction.

If you don't get relief from HR, you can always file an Equal Employment Opportunity Commission (EEOC) compliant. Remember, even after you leave a position under these circumstances, you have six months to file. Now, filing an EEOC complaint will increase the tension between you and the perpetrator, and sometimes even the organization, so be prepared for that. If you file, you are in a very serious place, so be prepared to fight. Oftentimes, grieved individuals simply make an exit plan and move on to the next opportunity. While this is good for that person, it does not solve the problem and I guarantee that someone will come under attack in the future. Your actions and willingness to take a stand could save someone else from facing a similar catastrophe.

As an unselfish leader, you must be cognizant of the fact that a new hire at your organization might be exiting a situation just described. Behind the smile is a broken person. A person who has been wounded and who is probably now in a fragile state. As humans, we are good at hiding what is really going on inside. This person will be vulnerable, and may be dealing with low self-esteem. The ability to trust others and have confidence in one's own abilities are in question. It is quite normal to be in a space like this when you have departed a hostile workplace. It is critical that you allow a new employee the opportunity to slowly grow comfortable with you and the team. Even the best of new hires can be overwhelmed quickly by a manager who thrusts them into the mix too quickly.

HR is a department created to place the company's priorities above any employee. Yet there are many great HR directors out there who believe that the employee is the most valuable asset a company has. They will ensure that the policies of the organization are adhered to regardless of a person's position, title, or longevity with the company. In other words, they understand that enforcing the company's policies, in turn, means protection of all employees. At a conference, when I laid out this process of dealing with a supervisor about whom you've got concerns, I was asked, "What do I do if none of this works?" I told the attendee, "Take your talents elsewhere."

Chapter 12
Coexisting

In our society, one of the greatest challenges is getting people to accept those who are different. Being able to value the experiences of others and accept an opposing viewpoint takes maturity and empathy. Different is not deficient; it's just different. Too often our differences are seen as barriers, which causes tension, fear, and mistrust. The media has played a critical role in defining who we are and what we are not. American history is laced with mistruths about race, culture, and identity. For the most part, it has not been a narrative of inclusivity, but of exclusivity. Our past is chronicled with sexism, racism, genderism, homophobia, and the like. We are a blended nation comprised of every nationality on this great planet, yet this is where the trouble began.

While this is not a historical account of those ills, it is worth mentioning that we are the greatest experiment to date. America is a heterogeneous society, but too many in our country claim a false homogeneous origin. They also claim that the current makeup of the country has corrupted this so-called purity. A simply cursory reading of American history debunks this notion. Again, we are a blended people, and moving beyond the false assertion that this country is the product of just one race is our greatest challenge. From the outset, we have been trying to coexist with little success. It is important that you understand as a leader that the societal factors impact the smallest of work groups.

Adding to these divisions is the flawed belief that any one particular group is monolithic. Within each ethnic group are varying degrees of similarities and differences. In addition, we also contend with geographical differences. As a black boy raised in Wisconsin by two parents and attending private

Catholic schools, I am sure that a black boy growing up in Alabama by a single mother and attending a segregated school would have a vastly difference experience. Yet in the eyes of many, because we share the same skin pigmentation, we are the same. As an unselfish leader, you must understand all of these differences and how they make us great. Yes, I say great because our differences are what makes this experiment one of the greatest in the world. As a country, we are strongest when we celebrate these differences. A company is more productive, possesses a healthy culture, and has a lower turnover rate when it celebrates the diversity of its workforce.

Whether you are in a leadership position or not, I want you to take a look at the people you work with. Let's look at the diversity:

Gender

_____

_____

_____

_____

Race

_____

_____

_____

_____

Age

_____

_____

_____

_____

Nationality

_____

_____

_____

_____

Geographical background

_____

_____

_____

_____

Sexual orientation

_____

_____

_____

_____

Work experience

_____

_____

_____

_____

_____

Education

_____

_____

_____

_____

Religion

_____

_____

_____

_____

Political views

_____

_____

_____

_____

_____

Take a moment and review your entrees. I hope that you're seeing a diverse work group. If not, this is a major problem. If you have a homogeneous workplace, then either your organization does not value diversity or your company is not a place where people outside of this collective makeup want to work. Either way, this is extremely problematic. However, if you see a range of diversity, then you have reason to celebrate.

Why do you have reason to celebrate this diversity?

_____

_____

_____

_____

_____

_____

For example, I have always celebrated various ethnic and cultural days with staff. We would put up a Cinco De Mayo display, send out emails honoring black Americans during Black History month, put up a Christmas tree, or participate in Hanukkah. These are beautiful celebrations that we can all learn from and appreciate. Our differences make us stronger and if we acknowledge and honor them, we are creating an environment where we coexist together.

Coexisting is defined as "exist[ing] at the same time or in the same place, especially in peace."[53] I want you to understand that existing means that we are present. That all of the "self" is present and fully recognized by others. When you don't feel valued, or you feel that you don't belong in that space, you are not present. You only reveal what you feel is acceptable to others. The sad truth is that many of us live in these spaces every day without being fully present. We have the fear of being judged, ostracized, and treated badly. When you don't trust those occupying the space you work in, you do whatever it takes to survive. Surviving is not thriving. Go to any workplace during the lunch period and you will see some of the most segregated times of the work day. Why is this?

Well, we desire to coexist; therefore, we gather with those who value us, those who we can trust, and those who don't judge us. This starts at an early age. We learn who those are that welcome us and those who reject us, beginning in pre-school. By the time we arrive in high school, we have clearly defined the spaces we are willing to participant in and the ones in which we are not. Through desegregation, our government has tried to forcibly overcome these tendencies. Keep in mind, it was our government that sanctioned segregation in the first place. You have people on both sides who agree and disagree with the methods of integration. This discussion is beyond the scope of this book; however, we are still dealing with a system

---

[53] Dictionary.com, s.v., "citation," accessed September 13, 2018, https://www.dictionary.com/browse/coexist?s=t.

that was designed to separate us and our challenge today is to continue to dismantle it.

If we truly exist at the same time and in the same space, we have created a healthy environment where all are accepted equally. While the inclusion is mandated by federal law, individuals must commit to the human ideas needed to produce the desirable outcome. A principle was enshrined in the U.S. Declaration of Independence that "all men are created equal," and I would add that women belong in this declaration. You should know this history as a leader, and be aware that we have yet to achieve equality. Your task is to be an example of this declaration and to instill in those you lead the importance of obtaining it. Now, it is impossible for you to achieve this on a global scale; however, you are positioned to succeed in this in your work circle.

One cannot coexist with others without acknowledging that we are all created equal. Equality is not based on one's socioeconomic status, race, gender, age, appearance, or sexual orientation. It is based solely on the fact that we are all born human, and at the end of the day, our humanity ensures that we view ourselves as part of the human experience. Not everyone you supervise will believe this axiom. Here lies the difficulty in creating a workplace where people can coexist. If the staff don't believe everyone is created equal, then you have a lot of work to do. Furthermore, just because people may accept this level of equality, that's no guarantee that coexisting will happen either. Most people will tell you that they are not a racist or that they "don't see color." By the way, "not seeing color" is racist. If you want to see me, you must see all of me.

I am trying to point out to you that coexisting has been a goal for many since the origin of our country. It has not been achieved in any measurable way - in or outside of the workplace. Yet this still remains our goal. A coexisting society or work environment means reaching beyond simply tolerance of each other. If I tolerate you, I am still seeing myself as the one in control. In other words, I am giving you permission to be in this space, and the uniqueness of you is allowed by me. Notice the power dynamic at play here. In a coexisting space, allowance is not a concept – only equality is. Now, a notion of superiority can be linked not only with the color of one's skin or one's socioeconomic status, for example. It can be associated with such factors as seniority, favoritism, job title, and the like. I once worked with a guy who felt, simply because he knew more about the day-to-day operations, that he was better than everyone else. Well, he *should* have known more since he worked there longer than anyone else. Did that justify his sense of superiority? Of course not.

Keep in mind that everyone who walks into your work space has had experiences that either encourage or discourage coexistence with fellow workers. From white privilege to discrimination, to sexism and others isms, we have all dealt with feeling less than equal, and some people have felt a sense of superiority because they are part of the dominant culture. An unselfish leader is keenly aware of the impact of history on those they lead. Given this knowledge, how do we create a blended team based on equality?

First, you accept the idea that each and all members of your team belong in that space. Regardless of their experiences up to this point, you acknowledge their innate value as human beings. You ensure that they are equally heard and seen. Your message is one of acceptance, and you address situations that challenge this principle. You are not trying to change the world at large; however, you are trying to change their world for the better. You treat every voice, idea, suggestion, or disagreement with equal weight. We will go into more detail about building teams in the final chapter. I suggest that you continuously train your employees on the concept of coexisting and the problems that prevent its successful implementation. I think employees should be evaluated on how well they coexist with others on the team. Thank employees for respecting and empathizing with others. Assign a person on your team to be the Coexistence Coordinator for new employees. If this becomes a corporate priority, you will create a company people don't want to leave. Above all, be a leader who exemplifies the philosophy of coexisting with those you lead and those you report to.

"Half a century ago, the amazing courage of Rosa Parks, the visionary leadership of Martin Luther King, and the inspirational actions of the civil rights movement led politicians to write equality into the law and make real the promise of America for all her citizens."- David Cameron

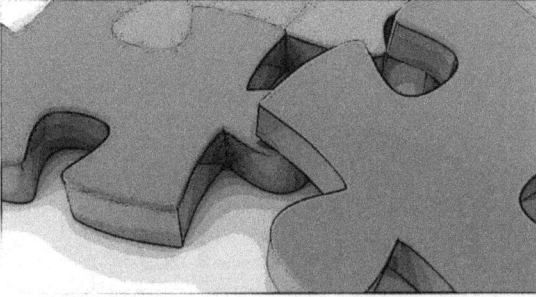

Chapter 13
Team Building

You could never be a leader if no one were following you. The most important aspect of leadership is the people. I think too many individuals in a leadership role miss this point entirely. Remember the guy I worked with who said the people who worked for him are like tools? If one breaks, you simply replace it. Although I heard this statement nearly two decades ago, I have never forgotten it. We were both department heads, and I immediately felt sorry for the people directly reporting to him. He did not understand that the greatest commodity as a leader were the ones he referred to as part of his proverbial toolbox. This is not a rare perspective in leadership. I would say that the majority of leaders don't understand that without people to lead, they serve no purpose.

Think of a coach that abuses his players. The coach's goal is to be successful and win. Do you think players who are abused will want to play hard for this type of leadership? Think of the jockey that abuses his horse. Will that horse perform at its highest potential when the race starts? I doubt it. As a leader, we are only part of a team. Every team needs a leader, but there are no one-person teams. We all have roles and responsibilities, and we depend on each other to perform in these capacities. Too many people are simply trying to get a paycheck to survive and as soon as a new opportunity presents itself, they're gone. Good teams don't lose people; they promote people.

I always advocate for children to participate in at least one group activity like sports, theater, or a chess or debate team. We need to learn how to work with others towards common goals. Working towards a common goal at an early age teaches selflessness. A problem with video games is that many are single player games. It is a zero-sum game. If I win, the "game" loses. There is value in sharing the victory as well as embracing the defeat. I remember when I was in 7th grade, our basketball team went 19-1 that year. We were undefeated as we entered the championship game. We ran up against a mighty St. Anne's team. The game came down to the last seconds and we lost. When we got to the locker room, our coach, whom we adored, was furious with us. He called us losers and chastised us for not winning. I recall being shocked and dismayed. After he stormed out of the locker room and we began to get over our shock, we all began to cry. Several minutes later, I turned to find my mother standing behind me. She asked me, "Why are you crying?" I thought that was a strange question, but before I would reply, she said, "Son, if you can learn how to win, you must also learn how to lose, and lose holding your head up." And then she said, "Get dressed."

My mother had so much wisdom. She had seen us rejoice all year long and had witnessed the sadness of those we defeated. I never really gave the other teams much thought after those victories. As a team, you win and lose together. You accept the outcome with dignity and you hold your heads up high. It's the same concept in the workplace. We either reach our goals together or we fail to reach them together. When we fail, we don't blame someone. We share the responsibility for our lack of success. A good team is hard to find and even more difficult to maintain. I was the MVP that year we lost the championship game. It was bittersweet not because we lost, but because of the way our coach treated us after the defeat. I vividly remember the locker room scene: I can see myself sitting on that bench, I can still see my teammates and the way we were facing each other; but above all, I can hear his rant.

As an unselfish leader, you are a coach and how you react to your team's performance can have lasting consequences for good and for bad. Your team will be a reflection of you. An angry coach produces an angry team. A condescending coach creates a condescending workforce. A manipulative coach builds a manipulative environment. Yet a wise and humble coach fosters an environment of growth, collaboration, and comradery.

It is important to note that building a strong team takes time, patience, empathy, love, and great leadership. There are specific levels in the building of a successful and competent team. The 6 levels are: *Skills, Defined Roles, Conflict, Acceptance, Trust, & Collaboration.* I encourage you to take the S.O.U.L. online course. I go into greater detail elaborating on each level. There is a Traditional way of executing each level, and there is the S.O.U.L. way. I will briefly talk about each of these.

In the Traditional Leadership approach, the *Skills* level is what I describe as what is required. In other words, you are expected to have all the necessary skills to do your job prior to being hired. The expectation is that you already know, and if you have to receive any instruction or direction, you are the problem. In the S.O.U.L. approach, the expectation is that you will be taught the skills you have yet to acquire. Therefore, instruction and direction are freely and openly offered by your supervisor and teammates. Remember, this is the first level. If teams don't embrace this approach correctly, they will never get to level 2. When I work with companies, I find that many of them have never left level 1. Supervisors tell me that their employees don't seem to have the skills necessary to get the job done. I ask them how long has this person been with the company? Often, I hear three or four months. It's taken everything for me not to laugh.

Once I was criticized for not knowing how to send the proper paperwork for ordering new company envelopes. I was newly hired and I asked one of my staff members how to get these ordered. She replied that she did not know. Keep in mind, she had been there for quite some time. So, I told her to call the marketing department and ask. To my surprise, I got a nasty email stating they were not a "copy max" and I needed to check with my supervisor. It turns out they had no procedure for doing this, and it took days for marketing to find the paperwork for me to fill out. My supervisor got angry at me because marketing contacted him. In this instance, I was required to know something that obviously very few people knew. In the S.O.U.L. approach, marketing would have told my staff member that there are forms for you to fill out, but it's been a while since we ordered any new ones, so as soon as we find them, we will let you know. A proper procedure would have been taught and not required. I cannot overly emphasize that many teams do not move beyond this point.

In the Traditional Leadership approach, *Defined Roles* are assumed. No one in the organization takes the time to discuss your roles and responsibilities with you. This happens a lot in fast-paced work environments. They pride themselves on getting things done. These are the jobs that describe position openings with, "must be able to work in a high-pressure job environment," or "must be able to meet deadlines under pressure." Who wants to work for a company that makes such claims? I served in the military, which is as high-pressure as they come, and even they didn't make such statements. In this type of work space, management is too busy to clarify roles. You are expected to know them, and I have found that most of the time, they could not articulate it to you if they tried. These teams are very dysfunctional. The supervisor allows everyone to do their own thing. These are very contentious and stressful organizations to work for.

In the S.O.U.L. approach, your *Defined Roles* are articulated. On your first day, you and your supervisor spend time outlining your role and how you fit into the overall picture. Your coworkers are informed of your role and how it correlates to their daily responsibilities. I have worked for several companies in which I never knew the role of other team members. When I specifically asked for the role they played, I was ignored or told to stay in my lane. What does that mean? This level is so important because without it, you can never collaborate with others. How can you possibly, if you don't know what they truly do or are responsible for? Think about how awkward it would be if basketball players did not know their roles out on the court during the game. It would be total confusion – and, yes, this would be true for any team. Without achieving this level, you will always have high turnover, confusion, and disillusioned employees.

In the Traditional Leadership approach, *Conflict* is a problem. Think about our previous chapter, *Coexisting*, and how difficult achieving this is. If you see conflict as a problem and not as an opportunity, people will never be accepted as equal. Conflict between human beings is inevitable. Whether in your personal or professional life, from time to time you will have disagreements. Again, we are not a monolithic people and neither do we see or react to the world in the same way. More often than not, employees are punished in some way for having conflicting views or for having strong opinions that differ from others. If you have no conflict at your workplace, your staff does not care. Listen: passionate and committed people care and sometimes conflict arises out of this tension.

In the S.O.U.L. approach, *Conflict* is seen as an opportunity for growth. It is not punished or looked down upon. Creating a space where conflict can be mitigated in a healthy way will make your team stronger. If you teach that every voice and opinion are valuable, people will not only express themselves, but hear the other person's point of view. Don't discourage your staff from embracing these moments. If you are working towards the same goal, have taught the proper skills to be successful, and everyone knows their role, working through conflict will only make your team more efficient. But if you see conflict as a problem, it will destroy your team.

In the Traditional Leadership approach, *Acceptance* is voluntary. This is where you hear people say, "I don't have to like you to work with you." This is such a callous statement, and why would you want to work with people that you don't like? These organizations live by a motto that's something like "Just get the job done." Why would you spend 40+ hours of your week simply trying to get the job done? That's 2,080 hours per year you spend with people you don't like. Furthermore, if you work 40 years, you will spend 83,200 hours simply getting the job done. I don't know about you, but I don't want to live my life this way. Everyone desire to be accepted and valued. When people are seen as dispensable or as a tool, accepting one another is not a priority. It is never about getting the job done, it is about how you do it. Are people involved, appreciated, happy, and empowered while working towards company goals? If not, acceptance is voluntary.

In the S.O.U.L. approach, *Acceptance* is expected. This is non-negotiable with an unselfish leader. Everyone, no matter their background or identity, will be fully accepted into the staff you lead. This is where an unselfish leader can shine. Be the example of acceptance. You should always place value in and give of your time to those newly hired and those who have been with you. Go out of your way to show appreciation and encourage them in all aspects of their lives. Be a coach and a mentor. Have you ever felt rejected or ostracized from those you work with? Are you sitting outside of the boss's work clique? It is not a comfortable feeling, so as leaders, we must ensure that no one is ever placed in such a position.

In the Traditional Leadership approach, *Trust* is undermined. This is a really tough one. It happens so often in the workplace. Trust is so fragile and at times, impossible to regain when lost. Distrust brings hurt and abandonment. This hurt causes one to question his own value. Oftentimes, we blame ourselves for the pain we feel when someone betrays us. Betrayal gives birth to trauma, and some of us are dealing with lifelong trauma. There is a lot of trauma in the workforce today. I have seen supervisors ruin the lives of those they were entrusted to care for. I have hired and worked with people whose brokenness has come from a previous supervisor or coworker. Without trust, there can be no success in our professional or personal lives.

Untrustworthy work environments are the most highly dysfunctional and destructive spaces to ever work in. I believe that no one should ever be betrayed on their jobs.

In the S.O.U.L. approach, *Trust* is valued. It is the highest currency in the workspace. Trust implies a sort of interdependence, and trust allows us to be vulnerable with each other. No one will offer a suggestion if she doesn't trust you. No one will disagree with you if she doesn't trust you. No one will let you beyond her walls of comfort if she doesn't trust you. Without trust, your organization will not be creative or take any risks. We always play it safe with people we don't trust. Being vulnerable allows for the true self to appear – unfiltered, confident, and willing to participate without reservation. As an unselfish leader, you are the epitome of trust. You give it and you expect it in return, but when trust is broken, you seek ways to restore it. In the online course, I go into great detail on how to restore trust.

Without mastering these previous 5 levels, you will never get to level 6, which is *Collaboration.* Great teams thrive in collaboration. They have the skills, they know their roles, they work through conflict, acceptance is key, trust is valued, and they embrace collaboration. All 5 levels are the foundation of collaboration. How can I collaborate with you if I don't know my role, or if I don't feel accepted, or most importantly, if I don't trust you? To reach your true potential as a team, you must learn how to collaborate. There is no "me" in collaboration. It is the "we" that counts. While the big projects come to mind when people speak of collaboration, for me, it's the small things. It's making a phone call, or following up on an email, or asking someone to improve your idea. Collaborating environments are happy ones. People love coming to work and they like the people they work with. It is more of a passion than a job.

Building a functional and efficient team is hard work. It takes a dynamic leader who understands that the team members are the most important assets. I want you to determine what level your team is on and why. How do you get to the next level? What does collaboration look like for your team? Take my online course to learn how to be an effective team builder.

Skills

_____

_____

_____

_____

_____

_____

Defined Roles

_____

_____

_____

_____

_____

_____

Conflict

_____

_____

_____

_____

_____

_____

_____

Acceptance

_____

_____

_____

_____

_____

Trust

_____

_____

_____

_____

Collaboration

_____

_____

_____

_____

The S.O.U.L is a new philosophical approach to leadership. After being in the United States Navy and in leadership for almost 30 years, I have seen what works. Not everyone will agree with the strategies you have learned in this book; however, they have never failed me. If you want to be a leader, you must remember how it felt to follow. Remember how it felt to follow a dynamic leader and more importantly, recall how it felt to follow a selfish leadership. The choice is yours; therefore, I say choose wisely... Be an Unselfish Leader.

Bibliography

Center for Creative Leadership, "4 Keys to Strengthen Your

　　Ability to Influence Others." Accessed September 13, 2018,

　　https://www.ccl.org/articles/leading-effectively-articles/4-

　　keys-strengthen-ability-influence-others/.

Collins, Richard F. "Mentorship as a Responsibility: Two

　　Thirties for One Fifty." *Journal of Environmental Health* 69,

　　no. 2 (September 2006), 4-13.

De Dreu, Crasten K.W. "The Virtue and Vice of Workplace

　　Conflict: Food for (Pessimistic) Thought." Journal of

　　Organizational Behavior 29, no. 1 (2008): 5-18.

Dictionary.com, s.v., " accessed September 13, 2018 – October

　　1, 2019, https://www.dictionary.com/.

Dreachslin, Janice L. "The Role of Leadership in Creating a

　　Diversity-Sensitive Organization." *Journal of Healthcare*

Management 52, no. 3 (May/June 2007): 151-154.

Harvard Business Review Press. *Performance Review.* Boston

    Massachusetts: Harvard Business School Publishing

    Corporation, 2015.

Holy Bible: New King James Version. Chicago: Moody Press,

    1985.

Hood, Jacqueline, "The Relationship of Leadership Style and

    CEO Values to Ethical Practices in Organizations," *Journal*

    of Business Ethics 43, no. 4 (April 2003), 263-273.

Kasperkevic, Jana. "HR is not there to be your friend. It's there

    to protect the company."

    https://www.marketplace.org/2017/10/30/human-resources-

    protect-employee-employer/.

McNamara, Brian, "Just Care More," *Talent Development.*

    (November 2018): 51-56.

Mitchell, Ted and Rao, Michael. "Mentoring and Peer

    Relationships: Two Young Leaders' Perspectives." *Change*

    30, no. 2 (January – February 1998), 46-88.

Morton, Johnnye L. and Grace, Marsha Grace. "Conflict

   Management and Problem Solving: Leadership Skills for

   the Reading Professional." *The Reading Teacher* 41, no. 9

   (May, 1988): 889-891.

Murphy, Michael, et al. "Stress and Organizational

   Culture." *The British Journal of Social Work* 26, no. 5

   (October 1996): 647-665.

O'Connor, Lydia. "Diversity is A Bunch Of Crap And Un-

   American,' Says GOP Congressional Candidate,"

   Huffington Post, June 11, 2018.

   https://www.huffpost.com/entry/seth-grossman-diversity-

   unamerican_n_5b1eaab9e4b09d7a3d7596f9.

Office of Performance Management. "Organizational Goals

   Can Be Powerful Energizers," https://www.opm.gov/policy-

   data-oversight/performance-management/performance-

   management-cycle/planning/organizational-goals-can-be-

   powerful-energizers/.

TechTarget, "Operational Goals,"

    https://searchcio.techtarget.com/definition/organizational-

    goals.

Webster, Martin and Webster, Vicky. "10 Signs of

    micromanagement — Strategies for Dealing With

    Micromanagers," Leadership Thoughts,

    https://www.leadershipthoughts.com/10-signs-of-

    micromanagement/.

Michael Eric Owens is President of M.E.O. Consulting and the Founder / Executive Director of the Ralph Ellison Foundation. He is a distinguished scholar, writer, and speaker. Following a successful career in the United States Navy where he achieved Sailor of the Year honors, he attended the University of Wisconsin-Parkside, earning degrees in History and Political Science and Law as well as the Outstanding Graduate Award. He received his Master of Library & Information Science from the University of Wisconsin-Milwaukee. Michael is the author of the notable book, *Yes, I AM, Who I Am: A New Philosophy of Black Identity.*

Throughout his career, Michael has held leadership positions in the military, manufacturing, legal, and non-profit arenas. He is a sought-after and powerful voice in the areas of leadership, organizational culture and goals, diversity & inclusion, conflict management, decision making, and many more topics related to building strong organizations.

Michael serves on the Oklahoma Civil Rights Commission Advisory Board and the Oklahoma City Arts Commission Board. He is a member of the University of Oklahoma's AFAM Board of Visitors. Michael was named 2013 Educator of the Year by Perry Publishing & Broadcasting. He has taught at Northcentral University and the University of Central Oklahoma. As a 21st Century Leader, Michael continues to develop and mentor a new generation of leaders.

For training or coaching inquiries, contact:
michael@meoconsultingllc.com